WEDDING CUSTOMS AND FOLKLORE

WEDDING CUSTOMS AND FOLKLORE

Margaret Baker

DAVID & CHARLES
Newton Abbot London Vancouver
ROWMAN AND LITTLEFIELD
Totowa, New Jersey

ISBN 0 7153 7325 0

© Margaret Baker 1977

Set in 12 on 12 Photon Bembo
and printed in Great Britain
at the Alden Press, Oxford
for David & Charles (Publishers) Limited
Brunel House Newton Abbot Devon

First published in the United States 1977
by ROWMAN AND LITTLEFIELD
81 Adams Drive, Totowa,
New Jersey 07512, U.S.A.

Library of Congress Cataloging in Publication Data

Baker, Margaret, 1928–
Wedding customs and folklore.

Bibliography: p.
Includes index.
1. Wedding customs and rites. I. Title.
GT2665.B34   392'.5   76–1937
ISBN 0–87471–821–X

Published in Canada
by Douglas David & Charles Limited
1875 Welch Street North Vancouver BC

CONTENTS

INTRODUCTION

Even late in the twentieth century, wedding folklore is still a force to be reckoned with: few weddings take place today without a deferential glance at old marriage customs and beliefs. When, about 1930, Sisley Huddleston described the emotions of a young couple marrying in his Normandy village, did he not write of universal feelings which guarantee long life to the traditional wedding?

> They wish to surround their union with every available kind of pomp. They feel that it should be consecrated, and made indissoluble by public proclamation. A wedding is not an everyday thing, to be conducted casually and coldly, without a cloud of witnesses. The marriage ceremony flatters their sense of their own importance, and of the importance of the contract into which they have entered. We all, at our hours, love to stand in the limelight, and to play our part as on a stage, and be admired and felicitated. For the ordinary man and woman marriage is the unique occasion of their lives to set themselves apart, and to command public interest and sympathy. Neither at their baptism nor at their burial will they be conscious, as they now are, of being more than human beings, of being exceptional persons, veritable gods. . . [1]

Some wedding practices of long pedigree reach back to the days of primitive marriage, whose influence is clearly visible in our modern ceremonies. Then, brides were obtained by purchase, capture, service (as Jacob gained his wives) or barter, with purchase and capture as leading methods. Wedding folklore rests squarely upon those beginnings. The proverbial hostility between mother-in-law and son-in-law, the roles of best man and bridesmaids, the honeymoon, all spring from marriage by capture. Marriage by choice arrived with Christianity and spread very slowly. Love and marriage were long to be separate states.

Among the Khond of India, bride-capture remains serious

A wedding in Normandy, about 1853. Riflemen stand ready to fire a protective volley into the air as the couple emerge from church (*Schweizerisches Museum für Volkskunde*)

enough. The women repulse the men with sticks and stones, but little by little the bridegroom's party reaches the bride. An observer wrote earlier this century: 'This fighting is by no means child's play, and the men are sometimes seriously injured.' Such aggression echoes the old Irish custom of 'dragging home the bride'. Then 'having come near to each other, the custom was of old to cast short darts at the company that attended the bride, but at such a distance that seldom any hurt ensued; yet it is not out of the memory of man that the Lord of Howth, on such an occasion, lost an eye,' an unfortunate accident still remembered in 1682.[2]

Before marriages based upon romance were commonly accepted, purchasing a wife was a tough business deal like any other. Although the world is now perfectly familiar with the emancipation of women, arranged marriages, in which the bride is not consulted, are still common, particularly in the eastern Mediterranean, India and the Far and Middle East, and spirited haggling beforehand establishes brideprice and dowry. It may be, of course, that these older ways should not be despised: sociologists have suggested that arranged marriages, supervised by parents and founded upon contracts, common-sense and cash are as likely to turn out as happily as those relying upon the Western ideal of 'romantic love'. In fact the marriage contract, in a broader, modern sense, with domestic responsibilities and property rights clearly defined, has become increasingly popular in the West.

Evil spirits, especially hostile to those at life's crossroads, traditionally have been considered to brood over bridal parties, and protective rituals and charms still abound, although today regarded lightheartedly enough and usually uncomprehended by their users. Malevolent yet dunder-headed demons were banished by the clash of bells and the rattle of gunfire: in the twentieth century, car-horns have joined the cacophony. An implied *fait accompli* recklessly invites attack: wise girls arrange proxies for wedding rehearsals. There is safety in numbers and disguises, so bride, maids, bridegroom, best man and ushers in wedding 'uniform' and of like age, still move in a compact group, as they did when the evilly-intentioned were given no opportunity to identify their victims.

About fifty years ago, in the West at least, marriage began to lose its age-old connection with childbearing. To wish a couple a large family today may be less than tactful. But when land was at stake and sons important for agricultural survival – still the case in some unmechanised communities – fertility might be established beforehand by trial marriage, with the useful dividend of revealing wifely responsiveness. A Cambridgeshire vicar calling to reprove a farmer's son for a bundling exploit was reminded tartly that he wouldn't dream of buying a horse without getting astride it to see how it trotted! Rice and confetti shower over the wedding couple: at every wedding food and flowers symbolise increase. Like will create like, even if ten children are no longer the form of increase desired by most couples.

At marriage, the bride and bridegroom change social groups and separation from the old life is marked by passage rites – engagement announcements in newspapers, farewell presentations at the office, the stag party. Incorporation into the new group follows – with encircling wreath and ring and shared wedding-cake. Luck-giving charms and amulets – the horseshoe and bride's garter among them – are intermingled with these rituals.

Many pleasing wedding customs described in this book are very much alive today, but others have slipped quietly away. By the late eighteenth century a greater sense of propriety was beginning to affect weddings, as other social life, and today we may see only pallid derivatives of formerly lusty rituals. Changes came in other ways too. In the Western world, for example, the movement to towns at the Industrial Revolution disposed of the week-long wedding feast, which became burdensome to host families cut off from country resources. Unsympathetic employers awaited at least some of the guests next morning and feats of wedding eating and drinking – once a fine joke – could now be disastrous: no one was fit for much after a 'silver bridal'.

In Europe, particularly, two wars in this century destroyed patterns of place and family. American fashions spread ever wider through films, television, servicemen and the worldwide circulation of such periodicals as *Bride's Magazine* and *Modern*

Bride, which gave young couples fresh ideas about the management of their weddings. Life's increasing conformity has been unsympathetic to folklore of all kinds, but wedding beliefs and customs concerning dress, flowers, bridecake, rings, guards of honour, bells and bridesmaids seem as vivacious as ever, even if nothing is heard now of dancing in hogtroughs, flinging stockings or invading bridal chambers. (Never again shall we see the parson bombarded with nuts.) With the odd tough exception (feet-washing comes to mind) the modern fear of looking foolish killed such horseplay.

Still, much remains. The love potion, spell and aphrodisiac are certainly with us: the best hope for the lovesick, vengeful and uncertain lies with old gods. Bouquets are thrown to select the next to marry; the 'shower' echoes the generous old bridewain; honeymoon destinations are close secrets; wedding bells peal out; trial marriage fits comfortably with contemporary ideas. The parades of potential brides at St Petersburg a hundred years ago, and frank advertisements for mates in the Boston newspapers of the eighteenth century, are matched today by computer dating, the matrimonial press, the marriage bureau – and in 1974, by the latest phenomenon, the German 'marriage market' television programme. Wedding folklore never stands still.

THE APPROACH TO MARRIAGE

LOVE POTIONS AND MAGIC

Love potions and philtres turn upon life's eternal problem of winning and holding the love of others. They were the dark stock-in-trade of Elizabethan and Stuart witches and their European and Eastern counterparts, experienced in trafficking in the affections as in other emotions, but when witchcraft began to fade in the seventeenth and eighteenth centuries, the ancient wisdom passed into the hands of gipsies, whose folklore is still rich in love spells, especially in Southern Europe. The southern United States has equally strong traditions; love magic is far from forgotten.

One typical gipsy love spell demands that the suppliant burn at a crossroads, at the moon's first quarter, a figurine moulded from the hair, saliva, blood and nailparings of the beloved. She must then urinate on the spot, repeating 'X—, I love you. When your image shall have perished you will follow me as a dog a bitch,' and her victim will come to enjoy no peace except at her side. An image named for a victim is immemorial magic: injury to the figurine is injury to the victim himself.

Implanting blood, sweat or saliva into a person induces love, just as the destruction of these substances destroys it. In rural Oklahoma, man wins woman by putting a drop of his blood on a candy for her to eat; woman governs man by similarly treating his whisky with menstrual blood, or by sprinkling his coat with alcohol into which has been pressed a piece of beef worn beneath her arm for two days. Sweat, like saliva and urine, is a powerful aphrodisiac and controlling agent: two sweets stuck together with sweat were said by the Scottish peasantry to give a man power over any woman he desired. A Norfolk poacher recalled forty years ago that a man desiring a girl's love had but to prick an orange all over with a needle and to sleep with it under his arm. Next day he must encourage the girl to eat the fruit, without explaining his gift: if this were achieved he could be sure that she would return his love. Such charms lured girls — willing or not — from their homes, as the Scottish ballad 'Fause Sir John and May Colvin' tells:

> Frae below his arm, he's pulled a charm,
> An' stuck it in her sleeve;
> And he has made her gang wi' him,
> Without her parents' leave.

The writer's great-grandmother, discovered working as a barefoot farm drudge about 1848 in County Cork, Ireland, by her future husband, maintained until her dying day that she had been lured from her wealthy home in the west of Ireland during the 'troubles' by tinkers using such a charm. She had found herself powerless to resist although well aware that it had been administered.

In Hungarian lore one of the least hurtful charms to secure a man's love uses the yellow roots of the *Orchis maculata*, gathered at midsummer, dried, mixed with menstrual blood and added to the food of the desired one. The potently phallic orchis ('dog-stones') has two testicle-like tuberous roots and by imitative magic to carry them brings virility and luck in love. In the Swiss Alps the 'man's troth' or nigritella, a vanilla-scented dark red orchis, is slipped under a boy's pillow to make him utterly besotted, or into a girl's apron pocket to cause her, however carefree, to fall hopelessly in love. In the southern United States, as in North Africa, the aphrodisiac vervain planted at the doorstep attracts lovers; the plant 'devil's shoestring', *Coronilla varia*, chewed and rubbed upon the palms, gives a man power over any woman with whom he later shakes hands. In the Ozarks, the would-be lover hid the dried tongue of a turtle dove (bird of love) in a girl's cabin and she could then deny him nothing. Distracted parents would search for days to find such dangerous charms. And disposal of the unwanted was not neglected. Southern negroes make it hot for an undesired lover by burying his 'tracks' — earth upon which his footsteps have fallen — in an anthill. Another notorious charm uses the tracks of man and wife. The earth is put in a paper-bag with whiskers of cat and dog and the whole flung into the fire. Henceforth the pair will be as antagonistic as these animals and the marriage will soon founder.

The jilted, too, do not suffer their fate meekly. In vicious vengeance, Slav girls secretly mix broken crabshell (a counter-aphrodisiac) with the food of a lover who has chosen another, to cause him to pine for his earlier sweetheart throughout a wretched marriage. And in Ireland the rejected girl buried a lighted candle in the churchyard at night. One recreant lover, a robust and healthy man, was seen to pine away: everyone knew that a 'candle had been buried against him' but no entreaty persuaded the girl to say where it lay. Eventually the candle was found and the man made to eat it to neutralise the curse, but the cure came too late, and he continued to languish and eventually died.[3] or a girl could bury in an anthill a sheep's testicles, named for the boy who had jilted her, and as they were consumed by the ants so would his virility humiliatingly diminish. The corresponding portion of an animal, named for the victim, and used with malignity, worked woe.

FUTURE PROSPECTS

To within the past sixty years, signs revealing the identity of future partners were keenly sought. Even in 1913 it was said of a list of Herefordshire divination charms that 'nearly all . . . are still practised, though not so firmly believed in as formerly'. Certain days and seasons favoured divination by the old magical formulae: the eves of St Agnes and St Mark; Hallowe'en (31 October, Old Year's Night in the Celtic calendar); and 30 April (eve of Celtic summer) were 'spirit nights' when the barriers between real and supernatural worlds were frail.

These charms, bringing excitement to dull lives, and half-seriously accepted, had no intrinsic effect upon events. Yet they cannot be dismissed as nonsense. In love as in other endeavours confidence and conviction play their parts, and a boy or girl with secret hopes confirmed by the outcome of a charm might be strengthened to bend events in the desired direction. The modern newspaper horoscope works in a similar way.

American apple-paring bee

In an Arkansas charm, 'the dumb supper' (derived from the
English 'baking the dumb cake'), bread of cornmeal, salt and
spring water, was baked by two girls who had neither spoken
(hence the name) nor eaten that evening. Future husbands
entered the room as phantoms, to turn the cake and it was
essential that kitchen doors and windows be stood open for
them to leave, or consequences would be dire. A word, laugh,
even a frivolous thought, destroyed the charm. Parents today
often forbid their daughters to meddle in such rituals, rightly
linking them with witchcraft; the procedure is certainly awe-
inspiring enough to induce hysteria in a highly-strung
adolescent. In a similar Moroccan charm the enquirer bakes and
eats a tiny highly salted cake which she kneads on her left thigh;
during the night the spectre of her future mate will appear with
water to quench her thirst.

Hemp or cannabis, today of sinister reputation, was a
respectable field crop a hundred years ago. Even then the plant
had curious qualities. Workers in hempfields complained of
headaches and women were never allowed to take part in the
harvest lest they become barren. It was the 'devil's flower' with
hallucinogenic virtue (well known to users today) and
consequently a high reputation as a raiser of spectres. In a charm
certainly practised until 1900, the suppliant scattered hempseed
as she walked through garden or churchyard on Midsummer
Eve, saying:

> Hempseed I set, hempseed I sow,
> The man that is my true love
> Come after me and mow.

And the ghostly form of her lover would appear after her,
mowing the crop with his scythe. As this was haytime, young
men carrying scythes were likely to be about the village by
night: a further explanation of a vision which ambitious lovers
were only too delighted to foster.

Nuts and apples have been magical from prehistoric times –
perhaps even from the Garden of Eden. Nuts named for lovers
were laid on a hot hearthstone at Hallowe'en to the rhyme:

Divination with nuts at Hallowe'en

If you love me, pop and fly,
If not, lie there silently.

In Wales grains of wheat, one for the boy, one for the girl, were set upon the fire and if they jumped from the shovel together the couple would 'bound into matrimony'. Round the school stoves of northern Ohio apple pips were used, with the subtle implication that if the girl's pip moved towards the boy's, she was fonder of him than he of her. At the sociable apple-paring bees of pioneer America (illustrated on page 15), girls threw unbroken parings over their shoulders hoping that they would fall in the shape of future husbands' initials.

Shirts and shifts, intimate garments assuming human form, had eerie qualities. George Wood, a farmer at Raynham, Norfolk, England, in the early nineteenth century, told of riding home late one Hallowe'en and seeing a light in his cartshed window. He peered in to see five silent men sitting round a pitchfork supporting a clean shirt, believing that the sweetheart of one of them, if faithful, would come to claim it.[4] About 1860 a girl performed this charm at Yarmouth, but thoughtlessly made her intentions public. During the night a sailor strode boldly in to seize her shift – which next morning was flying from the mast of a ship tied up at the quay. Unwelcome but ardent suitors were never above taking such excellent opportunities of presenting themselves as those selected by fate.

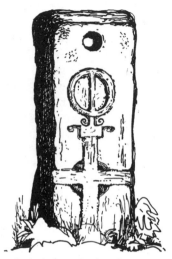

The holed stone of Inishmore, Aran

Standing stones and menhirs retain atavistic potency. On Aran, Ireland, a girl who passes her handkerchief through a hole in the stone of Inishmore quickly finds a lover. Almost to the present day single women travelled far to sit upon the huge granite *Clach-na-Bhan* – 'stone of the woman' – near Braemar, Scotland, or on the white 'pierre du bonheur' on the beach at Le Pollet, Normandy, to ensure the capture of a husband within the year. At the chapel of St Catharine (saint of spinsters) in the Forêt de Lyons, Eure, girls lay pins from a bridal veil before the saint's statue to induce swift marriage, and at Forcaray, Galicia, Spain, St Anthony's statue is carefully protected from girls who will tie a rope round the saint's neck and haul him into the rain if he fails to provide them with sweethearts. But if St Anthony obliges they gratefully knot their lovers' neckties about his neck. On one morning in recent years, the saint was found to be wearing no fewer than seven such ornaments!

ST VALENTINE'S DAY AND LEAP YEAR

The origins of the feast of St Valentine, saint of lovers, are obscure, but they may be linked with the Roman festival of Lupercal, celebrated about 15 February, on the spot where the wolf was said to have suckled Romulus and Remus. Then men drew girls by lot, as partners. When Valentine was martyred about 270 AD the early church attempted, with some success, to transfer the Lupercalian revels to the saint's feast.

Girls sometimes believed that they would marry the first bachelor they saw on 14 February and carefully avoided unacceptable candidates: Mrs Samuel Pepys, wife of the English diarist, covered her eyes all the morning on St Valentine's day, 1662, against the painters at work gilding the chimneypiece. Present-giving and lot-drawing were entertainments of the day. Henri Misson de Valbourg, a Frenchman who visited England about 1700, wrote:

> On the Eve of 14th of February, St Valentine's Day, a time when all living Nature inclines to couple, the young folks in England and Scotland too, by a very ancient custom, celebrate a little Festival that tends to the same end. An equal number of Maids and Bachelors get together, each writes their true or some feigned name upon separate billets, which they roll up, and draw by way of lots, the Maids taking the Men's billets, and the Men the Maids', so that each of the young Men lights upon a Girl that he calls his Valentine, and each of the Girls upon a young Man ... each has two Valentines: but the man sticks faster to the Valentine that has fallen to him, than to the Valentine to whom he is fallen. . .

These traditions were taken to America by the first English settlers, but the Puritans of New England frowned upon such frivolity: 'No lad shall attend a maid on the fourteenth of February,' ran one repressive declaration. Public expressions of affection were banned by law: Captain James Kemble returned

A valentine of 1820: a 'cheque' drawn on the Bank of Love, signed by Cupid (*Crown copyright: Victoria & Albert Museum*)

from a three-year sea voyage on 14 February 1764 and in a Boston street gave his wife a smacking valentine kiss: he was promptly sentenced to two hours in the stocks for unseemly behaviour.

Today valentine gifts are fully exploited commercially and heart-shaped boxes of chocolates, perfume, cakes and other presents appear in the world's shops early in February. Florists say that more red roses – emblems of love – are bought for St Valentine's day than for any other day of the year: a custom said to have begun in France when Louis XVI gave his queen, Marie Antoinette, red roses on 14 February. Towards the end of the eighteenth century, valentine cards – at first homemade, later stationers' confections of tinsel, lace and flowers – began to be sent anonymously to objects of affection. So heavy was postal traffic on St Valentine's day that in nineteenth-century London, postmen claimed a special allowance for meals to sustain them during their labours. The popularity of valentines has not decreased since then. The Duke of Portland's card to Betsey Keates in 1847 carried a romantic rhyme typical of many such tributes:

If you love I as I love you,
No knife shall cut our love in two.

In modern Cuba, St Valentine's day, favourable for all matters of the heart, is 'Loving Day', and the average number of weddings celebrated in the Palacios de los Matrimonios, largest of Cuba's 'wedding palaces', jumps from a normal thirty to well over one hundred.[5] The day constantly provokes fresh responses. On 14 February 1975, it was arranged that 120 British paratroopers, returning from duty in Northern Ireland, should jump into the arms of waiting sweethearts and wives, in a 'St Valentine's day lovers' leap'. The troops, sixteen at a time, parachuted down into a heathery field near Aldershot, Surrey. Identification of the falling figures was not easy! Two ambulances, engines running, stood by, but the only casualty was a wife who twisted her knee dashing over to her husband. The British Army, showing suitable poetic licence, called the jump 'a normal training operation'.

In a 'leap year' or 'ladies year', every fourth year, natural order is overturned and girls propose to men. In 1936 the British Post Office issued 'golden valentine telegrams' to assist such enterprises: thousands were delivered. If rejected in leap year a girl may claim a compensatory silk gown, and in 1288 the Scottish parliament issued a helpful ordinance, firmly stating the old usage in black and white:

> . . . for ilke year known as lepe yeare, olk maden ladye of bothe highe and lowe estait shall hae liberte to bespeke ye man she like, albeit he refuses to taik hir to be his lawful wyfe, he shall be mulcted in ye sum of ane pundis or less, as his estait may be; except and awis gif he can make it appeare that he is betrothit ane ither woman he then shall be free.

Similar laws were passed in France, Genoa and Florence. Even today it is said jokingly that no man is safe during a leap year: but if he *is* caught all will go well – 'Happy they'll be that wed and wive within leap year: they're sure to thrive'.

2

COURTING DAYS

TRIAL MARRIAGE AND BUNDLING

Sometimes virginity has been prized less highly than evidence of sexual experience, even of the ability to conceive. Until recent years, in the Japanese *mikka kasei* or 'three-day rent marriage', the bride, escorted by her party and the go-between, stayed for three days at the bridegroom's house. If the young people liked each other, a formal marriage might follow, or the couple merely continue to live together, but the whole experiment was arranged with such delicacy and tact that it could be quietly dropped without the least embarrassment to either party.

Handfasting was a custom of eighteenth-century Scotland. The couple lived together for a year and a day and if pleased with the arrangement could extend it for life. Some linked handfasting with the influence of the former Roman settlements in Scotland: under the Roman law of *usus* or prescription, if a woman lived for a year with a man without being absent from him for three nights, they were considered to be married. In an echo of another Roman marriage form, *confarreatio*, in which the couple shared a cake sitting side by side upon an ox yoke (typifying matrimony), in 1867 the *Liverpool Daily Courier* reported the case of a couple who had merely lived together, and yet registered their children as legitimate. They could not afford the marriage fees, so knelt and mixed handfuls of meal in a basin, swearing on the bible not to part until death, a ritual they felt to be as binding as marriage. And typical of other informal arrangements, a French gipsy woman still shatters a clay vessel before any man with whom she wishes to live and remains with him for as many years as there are sherds. They may then separate or make another contract by breaking another pot.

Agricultural communities naturally liked firm evidence of

fertility before proceeding with marriage. In rural France, the Scandinavian countries and Iceland, in particular, until comparatively recent years, peasant women commonly did not marry until they had given birth or were advanced in pregnancy. John Smeaton, the civil engineer, found similar customs among the quarrymen of the Isle of Portland, Dorset, in the mid-eighteenth century. They rarely sought brides off the island: 'if, after a competent time of courtship' a girl was not with child the couple separated, accepting this mark of fate's disapproval. Smeaton's London workmen, used to more carefree ways, quickly formed attachments to the Portland girls but were surprised to find public opinion so strident when they attempted to evade their responsibilities that they were threatened with stoning from the island. Censure was so effective that only one illegitimacy was reported.

Bundling, *queesting* or 'bed fellowship', when the young couple comfortably and (it was said) innocently, shared the same bed during lovemaking, was a premarital custom of Wales, the Hebrides, Finland, Norway, Holland, Switzerland, Northern Ireland and the eastern states of America: '. . . though British travelers have uniformly endeavoured to fix the odium of this custom upon us their transatlantic cousins, as being peculiarly "an American institution," it is, nevertheless, an indisputable fact that bundling has for centuries flourished within their own kingdom,' wrote an American historian in 1871. This was true. In Cheshire it was 'sitting-up' and couples spent the night together in houses or outbuildings left open for them. Farmers who refused this privilege found that they could not keep servants.

Girls were naturally reluctant to dismiss sweethearts to walk home across moor or mountain at the evening's end. In simpler homes, in any case, there was often little distinction between hearth and bed; lovers merely shifted their position a few feet to a heap of fern, straw and blankets in the corner of the kitchen. Bundling, encouraged by crowded, ill-heated homes, was not the only stratagem of lovers craving solitude. In the Connecticut Valley sweethearts spoke to each other privately across the family hearth, through a long hollow 'courting stick' fitted with mouth and ear pieces.

New England courting stick

When bundling, girls fastened their petticoats with a sliding knot to at least delay, if not prevent, liberties: a traveller in Ireland in 1807 spoke of 'this extraordinary experiment which often ends in downright wedlock – the knot that cannot slide'.[6] (There was much talk of knots: 'to tie a knot wi' the tongue, at yan cannot louze wi' yan's teeth' was a discouraging Yorkshire assessment of marriage.) A Welsh mother with a daughter approaching the bundling age produced a 'bundling stocking', which, like single-legged pyjamas, completely enveloped the girl's body from the waist downwards: these garments, often family heirlooms, were in use until the late nineteenth century.

On the Dutch islands of Vlieland and Texel parents entirely approved of *queesting*, when lovers slipped beneath quilts with their daughters. Winter economy in firewood and candles far outweighed chastity. In Switzerland about 1860, bundling was practised as *dorfen, stubetegetren*, or *lichtgetren* ('going a-wooing') or in Canton Lucerne, as *kiltgang*. Urchins pelted the embarrassed lover on his way to call upon his sweetheart and serenaded the couple with teasing cat-voices until he crept out at dawn. Caterwauling invariably accompanied courtship.[7]

Emigrants carried these cheerful customs to the United States. Lieutenant Anbury, a British officer serving during the American Revolution, wrote of bundling in a letter of 20 November 1777 from Cambridge, Massachusetts. He had arrived at a small log hut for the night: there were only two beds and he asked where he should sleep:

> ' "Mr. Ensign," said the old woman "our Jonathan and I will sleep in this, and our Jemima and you shall sleep in that". I was much astonished at such a proposal, and offered to sit up all night, when Jonathan immediately replied, "Oh, La! Mr.

Ensign, you won't be the first man our Jemima has bundled with, will it, Jemima?" when little Jemima, who, by the bye, was a very pretty, black-eyed girl, of about sixteen or seventeen, archly replied, "No, father, not by many, but it will be with the first Britainer" (the name they give to Englishmen). In this dilemma what could I do? The smiling invitation of pretty Jemima – the eye, the lip, the – Lord ha' mercy. . . '

But the lieutenant decided that he could not trust himself and did not bundle after all.[8]

Bundling really ended with the improved housing of the later eighteenth and early nineteenth centuries, which meant that bed was no longer the only comfortable place for courting. In the United States at least, its end was accelerated by the publication in 1785 of 'A New Bundling Song; Or a Reproof to those Young Country Women who follow that reproachful Practice' whose author pointed out, with truth:

> . . . bundler's clothes are no defence,
> Unruly horses push the fence . . .

'A Poem Against Bundling. Dedicated to Ye Youth of both Sexes', a similar blasting by a clergyman of Bristol County, Massachusetts, declared that bundling reduced man to the level of the brutes, for:

> Dogs and bitches wear no breeches,
> Clothing for man was made,
> Yet men and women strip to their linen,
> And tumble into bed.

and roundly condemned bundlers and their games:

> Down deep in hell there let them dwell,
> And bundle on that bed:
> There burn and roll without control,
> 'Til all their lusts are fed.

But the defenders of bundling, as of all pleasant customs, were not silent. 'A New Song in Favour of Courting' spoke warmly of its highly practical *raison d'être*:

Man don't pretend to trust a friend,
To choose him sheep and cows,
Much less a wife which all his life
He doth expect to house.

Many years later practitioners were to recall bundling with
nostalgic affection. Colonel H., a native of Berlin, Connecticut,
born in 1775, told how mothers called in upon bundling couples
in bed to 'tuck 'em up and put on more bedclothes' and said that
'there wasn't any more mischief done those days than there is
now.' Another, jokingly asked by a grandson if he were not
ashamed of past exploits, asseverated: 'Why, no! What is the
use of sitting up all night and burning out fire and lights, when
you could just as well get under kiver and keep warm: and,
when you get tired, take a nap and wake up fresh, and go at it
again? Why, dammit, there wasn't half as many bastards then as
there are now!'

Bundling was found among the Pennsylvania Dutch as late as
1845; in New England, Cape Cod held out longest. One man
recalling his long bundling career there, spoke of finding his
sweetheart 'nicely snuggled under the bed clothes, having
previously put on a very appropriate and secure night dress . . .
like a common dress . . . furnished with legs, like drawers . . .
drawn at the neck and waist with strings tied with a very strong
knot . . . '. It would seem that not only bundling, but a version
of the bundling stocking also crossed the Atlantic!

ADVERTISING FOR BRIDES

On 28 May 1797 the English newspaper *Bell's Weekly
Messenger* carried the following advertisement:

'May no miscarriage prevent my marriage'
Matthew Dawson, in Bothwell, Cumberland, intends to be
married at Holm Church, on the Thursday before Whitsuntide
next, whenever that may happen, and to return to Bothwell to
dine.
Mr. Reid gives a turkey to be roasted; Ed. Clementson gives a
fat lamb to be roasted; Wm. Elliot gives a hen to be roasted; Jos.
Gibson gives a fat calf to be roasted.

And, in order that all this roast meat may be well basted, do you
see Mary Pearson, Betty Hodgson, Mary Bushley, Molly Fisher,
Sarah Briscoe, and Betty Porthouse, give, each of them, a
pound of butter.
The advertiser will provide every thing else for so festive an
occasion
   And he hereby gives notice,
TO ALL YOUNG WOMEN desirous of changing their
condition, that he is at present disengaged; and advises them to
consider, that altho' there be luck in leisure, yet, in this case
delays are dangerous; for, with him, he is determined it shall be
first come first served.
   So come along lasses who wish to be married
   MATT. DAWSON is vex'd that so long he has tarried.

This saucy invitation was matched by notices in American
newspapers. The *Boston Evening Post*, 23 February 1759, for
example, contained this appeal:

   To the Ladies. Any young Lady between the Age of Eighteen
   and twenty three of a Midling Stature; brown Hair, regular
   Features and a Lively Brisk Eye; Of Good Morals & not
   Tinctured with anything that may Sully so Distinguishable a
   Form possessed of 3 or 400£ entirely her own Disposal and
   where there will be no necessity of going Through the tiresome
   Talk of addressing Parents or Guardians for their consent: Such
   a one by leaving a Line directed for A.W. at the British Coffee
   House in King Street appointing where an Interview may be
   had will meet with a Person who flatters himself he shall not be
   thought Disagreeable by any Lady answering the above
   description. N.B. Profound Secrecy will be observ'd. No
   Trifling Answers will be regarded.

The demanding advertiser was said to be no more than an
impecunious subaltern in the British Army.

TOKENS OF LOVE

But most courtships moved more sedately along the slow and
sure path of meeting, wooing, gifts, betrothal. Love gifts were
many. The Irish 'harvest knot', Scottish 'brooch' and English

Harvest knots: love tokens from rural Ireland (*National Museum of Ireland*)

'countryman's favour', of plaited cornstalks, was a favourite
mark of admiration, made by village boys at harvest-time.
Grains were left upon tokens to be worn by girls; each was
analogous to a baby to come. The Northamptonshire wooing
token at sheepshearing was a fragrant 'clipping posy' of cabbage
roses, pansies, larkspur, honeysuckle, wallflowers, snapdragons,
gorse ('when gorse is out of bloom, kissing's out of season')
lavender and lad's love, bound with sweetbriar and ribbon
grass. Lad's love or southernwood, *Artemisia abrotanum*, aromatic
plant of cottage gardens, was a powerful courting aid. (Artemis,
or Diana, had special watch over women.) A shy suitor
presented a sprig to the girl of his choice; if she threw it down,
his hopes were dashed, but acceptance meant the start of their
first courting stroll. Honeysuckle was never brought indoors by
parents lest its rich, drowsy scent give their daughters erotic
dreams (in Germany the lime flower was similarly banned) but
this quality made the plant valuable to lovers. Sussex boys
bound a honeysuckle bine round a hazel stick and when after
several months the wood was twisted like barleysugar, its

possession gave instant success in courtship.[9]

Until perhaps 30 years ago gifts of clothing between engaged couples (at least until near the wedding) were generally frowned upon and called 'forward', a view perhaps deriving from the ancient significance of garments as gifts. In some European countries (and among the Bedouins) a girl may still reject any suitor she pleases, until she has accepted a gift of clothing from him; then there is no turning back. She is bound to give him every favour. In Scotland the handsewn 'wadding sark' or shirt was the bride's gift to the bridegroom, with significance going far beyond the bride's demonstrated skill at needlework. One peasant remarked that he never really intended to take Maggie (his wife) but 'the cutty saw this, flew to his neck and measured him for the sark, and so he was obliged to have her.' The sark's acceptance was a binding pledge of marriage. Even today in America it is reckoned unlucky for a girl to knit her boyfriend a sweater, some say because anticipation of housewifely duties tempts providence: more probably it is a confused recollection of the older belief.

Many useful presents were given during courtship. Cake moulds, butter prints, spoons and other wooden articles were finely carved by Pennsylvania Dutch, Swiss and Scandinavian peasants, both in their native lands and after emigration to the United States. Long-handled smoothers for the feathers of the bridal bed, pincushions (pins arranged in an affectionate message) or heart-shaped snuff and trinket boxes were exchanged. A carved stay-busk (or corset stiffener) in the Pinto Collection of Wooden Bygones at Birmingham Museum, England, has this typical love-gift inscription:

> When this you see
> Pray think of me
> The many miles
> We distant be
> Altho' we are a great way apart
> I wish you well with all my heart.

And about 1936 a visitor to a Swiss chalet high in the mountains was shown cupboards full of old family crockery with such loving legends as 'Mein ganzes Leben sei dir ergeben' – 'My whole life is dedicated to you'.

In the knitting regions of Europe a favourite gift was a needle sheath of bone or wood which hooked on to the knitter's skirtband to support one needle while she worked. Sheaths and needles had pleasingly erotic significance for both giver and receiver. The symbolism is plain enough. In northern France sheaths often bear an acorn decoration, perhaps remembering the importance in the Celtic world of certain oak trees under which marriages were celebrated. The early church had banned such paganism but newlyweds, seeking the best of both worlds and deprived of marriage under the tree itself, hurried from church to oak to dance three times round it and to carve a cross upon its bark. A 'marriage oak' – and a vague belief in its good-luck properties for bridal couples – survived at Brampton, Cumberland, England, until the nineteenth century.

In lacemaking districts bobbins were sometimes made from bones saved from the wedding feast, turned and decorated with incised lines and mottoes stained black or red: in the English Midlands decorative spots or lines of pewter made 'tigers' or 'leopards'; a small bobbin moving freely within a larger, a 'mother and child'. Inscriptions reflected the tensions of love:

> Sweet is the love that meets return but bitter
> When it meets a frown
> Richard Cobb slited by one A.S.

> You are the sweetest girl this village does
> afford and you don't love me – Aaron Lord.

And from those for whom matters were going more happily:

> Don't I love my Nance
> Kiss me quick my mome is comin[10]

Blown-glass rolling pins filled with salt, love tokens almost too frail for kitchen life, hung over doorway or fireplace to keep witches away. Thomas Ratcliffe of Worksop, Nottinghamshire, wrote of rolling pins in the English Midlands: 'One which hangs in a cottage near me bears the words "I wish you well". It was sent to the owner on her wedding day fifty years ago, and has hung on the same cottage wall for the whole number of years, used however, now and again, for special occasions in preparing pastry, for weddings and birthdays only.'

A pale-blue clouded-glass pin of great beauty, bought in Guernsey in the Channel Islands in 1878 and made for a sailor sweetheart's cabin, bore a wreath inscribed 'Love and Be Happy', a ship under sail, and the verse:

> From rocks and sands and barren lands,
> Kind fortune keep me free,
> And from great guns and women's tongues,
> Good Lord deliver me.

The purchaser, reflecting upon his impending marriage and upon his yacht's recent escape from the Casquets rocks in fog, felt his acquistion to be timely!

A cowhorn spoon from Canton Aargau, now in the Schweizerisches Museum für Volkskunde, Basel, is inscribed 'Kein Tropflein Blut in mir soll falsch sein gegen dir' – 'no drop of my blood can be false to you'. In Wales suitors carved wooden love spoons during long winter evenings and hearts, dates, initials, keys and keyholes ('you unlock my heart') expressed a shy lover's thoughts. The number of bowls the spoon had (one maker with soaring reproductive ambitions made a spoon with eleven bowls) showed the number of children a man desired.

BETHROTHAL AND THE ENGAGEMENT RING

Betrothal, the formal engagement, anticipated matrimony's irreversibility. Under Roman law the bridegroom furnished security for the completion of the bargain and the ring and solemn embrace gave the act mystic significance. 'Returning the ring' is still a vital step in breaking an engagement. Guernsey betrothals were marked by 'flouncing', a party at which the pair met friends of their parents-in-law to be. From this point it was unseemly for the girl to as much as walk with another male and the young man dared scarcely speak to another girl, even if

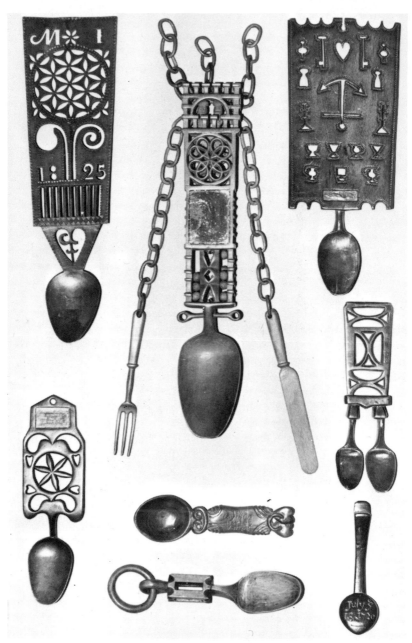

Welsh love spoons from the Pinto Collection of Wooden Bygones
(*Birmingham Museum & Art Gallery*)

Wedding rings: a Jewish ring (top left); an Irish Claddagh ring (top right); a posy ring (lower left); a gimmal ring (lower right)

courtship lasted for years. If the girl changed her mind after 'flouncing', her fiancé could lay claim to half her property; if he recanted she could do likewise. The early Christian church had similarly recognized the property implications of betrothal: *De Sponsalibus et Donationibus ante Nuptias* required a contract sworn before witnesses; if either party died during the engagement the survivor and heirs divided the estate between them. In old China, betrothal was so significant that if one (even both) of the pair died, the wedding ceremony went ahead as though nothing had happened; a girl once betrothed was treated like a widow. Actions for 'breach of promise' in which jilted sued jilter brightened English law courts until changes in the law a few years ago made such retaliation impossible. These actions had survived from a time when the undertaking to marry was of greater import than it is today.

An engagement ring marks the modern betrothal. From the Elizabethan period and earlier the gimmal ring, breaking into three parts – one for the woman, one for the man, one for the witness – and reunited later as the wedding ring, was well liked. Gemmed rings were not usual: gold or silver, perhaps twisted into a lovers' knot, were chosen, and not until the nineteenth-century exploitation of South African diamond deposits did white diamonds (of apposite durability: 'diamonds are forever,' say the jewellers: *diamond* comes from the Greek *adamas*, 'impenetrably hard') become both cheap and popular. In the eighteenth and nineteenth centuries precious stones whose initial letters spelled such words as 'dearest' (diamond, emerald, amethyst, ruby, epidote, sapphire, turquoise), 'love me' (lapis-lazuli, opal, verd antique, emerald, moonstone, epidote) or in France 'regard', 'souvenir' or 'amitié' made popular rings, still sought after in antique shops. The fiancé's birthstone is a luck-bringer in an engagement ring. Birthstones vary from country to country, but common dedications are:

January	garnet	July	carnelian, ruby
February	amethyst	August	sardonyx
March	bloodstone	September	sapphire
April	diamond	October	opal
May	emerald	November	topaz
June	agate, pearl	December	turquoise

Gemstones have their own virtues; turquoise helpfully prevents matrimonial arguments; emerald brings success in love; diamond denotes innocence and light; ruby preserves chastity; sardonyx ensures married happiness; topaz signifies fidelity; amethyst, sincerity; bloodstone, courage; garnet, truth and constancy. In America today there is a taste for jade, sapphire and emerald engagement rings but silvery pearls, symbolizing tears, and opals (most unlucky except for the October-born), fragile and unstable and showing changing colours (undesirable attributes for the betrothed), are avoided. German brides neutralised the ill-effects of pearls by wearing them in a tiny concealed casket – the gegentränen – 'averter of tears'. It is of course ill-omened to lose or damage an engagement ring, lest the contract it represents should suffer, and if another girl tries on the ring the owner's future happiness will be jeopardized.

3

THE MARRIAGE CONTRACT

In early times fathers had an undisputed right to dispose of daughters to the highest bidders; old phrases recall these hardheaded rituals, in form if not in spirit; a young man asks a father 'for his daughter's hand in marriage'; the latter 'gives the bride away'. But times are changing. On New Year's Day 1975, the age-old ritual came to an end at weddings of the Church of Wales. The Rev Elwern Thomas, Warden and Rector of Ruthvin, and a member of the Liturgical Commission which had recommended the new marriage service, said: 'our aim has been to get rid of the idea of a woman being a chattel at the disposal of her family'. The word 'obey' has been removed from the vows and while the bride's father still escorts her to church he is no longer formally asked to 'give her away'.[11]

In some societies (China, India, Africa, the Moslem world and sections of the Jewish community among them) marriages arranged by parents remain commonplace. This is not considered mercenary; is it not a father's duty to settle his children as favourably as possible? Physical attraction between the pair does not matter much, but it is important that brideprice, and dowry be thrashed out, often with lawyers' help. Social position, politics, religion and property have all in their time been influential in arranged marriages. Only the poor might marry for the luxury of love alone: a girl has always become prettier with a comfortable dowry of cows – or the cash equivalent, 'dry money'; 'a blanket is better for being doubled' might be the slogan of marriage negotiators.

If settlement cannot be reached through negotiation, romance does not normally prevail, although love matches are, of course, sometimes translated into happy marriages with the aid of bargaining. Parents take charge: in villages of North China, Fukien and Kiangsu about 1946, it was found that in 360 marriages, the agreement of only one young man had been sought beforehand: no brides were consulted.[12] It was felt positively foolhardy to allow children to seek their own mates. In the Moslem world many young couples still do not even meet before the wedding.

Despite modern liberalisation in many parts of the world chastity improves a girl's marriage chances. Anneline Kriel of South Africa, Miss World 1974, pointed out that there 'It is important for a girl to be a virgin when she marries.' In Brazil a girl minus virginity has little hope of marriage at all; in Morocco a bridegroom will pay from $70–$100 for a virgin, a mere $30 for a widow. In the West where the whole issue is far less emphasised, girls are nevertheless strongly urged by the more traditional women's magazines, and by parents, to avoid intercourse before marriage lest they 'cheapen' themselves and damage their bargaining power. The implications are plain.

Bargaining and wedding may more or less mingle. At an Orthodox Jewish wedding in New York a few years ago, Marcia Seligson found the *ketubah* or marriage contract under animated negotiation, by rabbis, bridegroom, fathers and witnesses, while the bride in full wedding finery waited patiently next door. The document specified her virginity and, among other things, the payments she would receive if widowed or divorced. Two hours passed in haggling, then suddenly a great shout went up — the *ketubah* had been signed! The groom danced in to claim his bride and the marriage ceremony could at last begin.

Marriage negotiations have taken many picturesque forms, including the 'choosing of brides' on Whit-Monday at St Petersburg, Russia, in the nineteenth century, when sons and daughters of citizens assembled in the Summer Garden to see and be seen. It was a brilliant display. Girls in best clothes were marshalled along the flower beds by their mothers. To show marriage-worthiness every possible ornament had been collected from mothers' and grandmothers' wardrobes: many girls were so laden with gold and jewellery as to be almost hidden from view. One mother, contriving further additions to her daughter's toilette, made a necklace of six dozen gilt teaspoons, a girdle of tablespoons and arranged punch ladles behind in the form of a cross. Evidence of solid wealth was vital. Young men in best caftans were conducted by their fathers through the rows of girls while parents expatiated on candidates' merits, mothers answered questions about dowries, fathers about prices. Eight days later searching interviews began, and after much consideration, notes were sent to the selected young people and couples were betrothed.

The dowry (the lump sum brought to the marriage by the bride) is still relevant: many French and Italian parents save for it from their daughters' earliest years. Serious problems existed, and perhaps still exist, for the dowryless. One of St Nicholas's prime works of charity was the provision, from his fortune, of dowries for three impoverished (and thus imperilled) daughters of a Patura nobleman. Portionless girls' chances of marriage were slim indeed and fathers of sons felt that desirable daughters-in-law came provided with the essential appurtenances. A practical solution in rural France fifty years ago, if the bride's family were very poor, was for a public collection to be taken up for the dowry or *dot*: donors received a kiss and a glass of wine from the pretty girls who made the collection. A father's first duty was to provide the dowry; if he died, the responsibility fell upon the brothers of the family. About 1890 Lucy Mary Garnett, a visitor to Turkey, was advised to avoid a certain young lawyer as 'not nice'; but the community nevertheless gave him full marks for striving to accumulate dowries for his orphan sisters. He had married one girl off with both dowry and dignity and was now working hard for the second.

Enterprising girls did not necessarily rely upon hard-pressed parents for endowment. In the nineteenth century thrifty girls from the Greek and Turkish islands worked as servants on the mainland and wore their savings as massive coin necklaces, excellent advertisements to prospective suitors and go-betweens. In pioneer countries a dowry was not always in coin: in America it might be a feather bed, valuable indeed, and Dutch Manhattan brides wore to the altar as many petticoats as they could carry, to demonstrate comfortable wealth. But all in all, cash was the usual provision: Judge Samuel Sewall's wife, Hannah Hull, daughter of Captain John Hull, the New England mintmaster of the seventeenth century, received as dowry her own weight in silver 'pine-tree shillings', and a London tradesman in the eighteenth century disposed of his eleven daughters giving to each girl her own weight in halfpennies. They were not sylphs. The lightest received £50 2s 8d! The other traditional marriage payments are far from forgotten.

A brideprice or *kalym* of from £4,000 to as much as £16,000 (say $7,000 to $28,000) is demanded in the remote central Asian republic of Turkmenia. Better educated, prettier girls fetch the best prices, although education only to about the age of twelve is required; highly educated women are said to make poor wives and, more important, to be less amenable to husbands' discipline. Girls cannot evade the system; in the past elopement has meant pursuit and stoning to death, with the girl's mother throwing the first stone, and it is not entirely certain that this punishment has died out in remote villages untouched by law. For families with several sons, assembling brideprices may be wearisome; if the price is paid in instalments to ease the burden, the bride returns to her father after the honeymoon and does not meet her husband again until the full sum has been handed over.

In Macedonia, girls are greatly outnumbered by men, and so although the sale of brides is now of course forbidden by law, eligible girls nevertheless command high prices. In 1974 one man complained to President Tito that a prospective bridegroom must pay to the girl's father between 40,000 and 60,000 dinars (some £1,340 to £2,000) before a wedding can be arranged, and a further 40,000 dinars in gold later. The letter reached the cabinet of the Macedonian State Government, but a spokesman said that the problem cannot further be solved by legal means, since the practice – acknowledged to be widespread is already outlawed. Nothing but a shift in social attitudes will resolve it.

Throughout marriage negotiations the go-between is still likely to be an influential figure. Until about 1850 in the isolated Plougastel peninsula, Brittany, when a marriage offer was on the table, two 'bazvalans' or intermediaries visited the bride by night: her mother showed approval of the union by her willingness to light a fire for the emissaries and they began a glowing – and not entirely truthful – account of the wealth and charms of the applicant. 'Lying like a bazvalan' is an old Breton saying. For form's sake they first refused the girl's mother and grandmother, jocularly offered to them before the bride was produced. The go-betweens, in odd stockings of red and purple, with white rods of office, later escorted the lover to visit his sweetheart and the couple ate from the same plate, sealing the contract. (Eating together was a binding ritual; in pioneer America a girl and boy eating from the same trencher were considered engaged.) If this portentous meeting was interrupted, the couple's children would be born crosseyed and humpbacked.

In the East one of the go-between's duties was to select astrologically compatible marriage partners. For 2,500 years Chinese marriage adhered strictly to the *Li Chi*, the Book of Ritual and Ceremonies. A girl's personal data were collated with the boy's; if her birth was on a day ruled by the tiger, and his was ruled by the dog, tiger devoured dog; a fire symbol in her name destroyed the wood symbol in his, and so on. But if the match was favoured by elders, difficulties were expeditiously brushed aside and the signs pronounced propitious. In Japan, until at least the 1930s the family asked a *naishōkiki* – 'secret finder-out' – to seek an eligible girl for their son. A semi-secret meeting was arranged for the young people; boy and parents visited a friend's silkworms as the friend's daughter (the selected girl) tended them, or the young couple appeared, chancelike, at the same healing spring. Like the three-day rent marriage, so tactful an arrangement could be dropped without embarrassment if reactions were unfavourable. Nothing was said openly. But if the young people responded, a *nakaudo* or go-between superintended further negotiations, performed the marriage ceremony and was responsible for the welfare of the union.

TROUSSEAU AND WEDDING PRESENTS

A bride may spend a lifetime assembling her trousseau – the linens, clothing and household goods which she brings to the marriage, which were once seen as partial compensation for the brideprice. The word derives from the French *trousse*, or bundle. In pioneer America, Wales, Holland, Scandinavia, Normandy and elsewhere, these goods were stored in the marriage chest, often an object of great beauty, represented today by the far simpler 'hope chest'. When Katharine Van Burgh married Philip Livingston in Manhattan about 1700, she provided a complete set of china from Delft, which was stored in a Dutch oak chest, twelve feet high, broad in proportion, compartmented for linen and silver and filled with secret drawers, its keyhole concealed among carvings. Comparable furniture was found in Yorkshire. In *Fifty Years in a Moorland Parish*, Canon J. C. Atkinson wrote of Danby-in-Cleveland:

> When I first came into residence here about 1850 there were few farmhouses in which there was not one of those fine old black cabinets or wardrobes with carved panels, folding-doors and knobby feet ... And not once or twice only but many times, I have heard the name 'bridewain' attributed to them. This seems to have been regarded as a usual part of the wedding presents.

A Pennsylvania Dutch bridegroom presented his bride with the traditional 'bride's box', oval and about eighteen inches long, of a size to hold the smaller trousseau items such as handkerchiefs. Stiffly conventional brides and bridegrooms whose stolid expressions belied emotional inscriptions such as 'Ich lebe dich mit Lust' with pomegranates of fertility and doves of happiness, were favourite painted decorations.[13]

Household linen has always been a staple trousseau item. When about 1930 Llewelyn Powys visited a Swiss bride-to-be near Glarus, he found her and her sisters industriously embroidering the wedding sheet with emblems of love. A lifetime's supply of trousseau tablecloths, napkins, towels and counterpanes was stacked nearby. In the nineteenth century a Turkish Osmanli bride departed for her new life with a great assortment of mattresses, pillows, quilts, sheets, copper kitchen utensils, furniture, a brazier and small items such as silver-mounted dustpans and trays elegantly inlaid with mother-of-

A Pennsylvanian bridal chest, c 1780, Berks County type. Decorations include doves (*Metropolitan Museum of Art, Rogers Fund, 1923*)

pearl. The trousseau dominated the thoughts of Italian girls from infancy. Petticoats, nightdresses, underwear of all kinds, embroidered and trimmed with rich lace, were counted in sixes of dozens if the bride were well-to-do and the peasant girl who could not count articles for her *corredo* in dozens was poor indeed.

Wedding gifts needed careful thought or they might do more ill than good. In pioneer America a bread peel, redolent of harvest, was a lucky present. Everywhere sharp or pointed objects were banned lest they 'sever' the romance, although this stigma could be dealt with. The *Worcester Herald* for 1858 reported that villagers had presented a squire's daughter upon her marriage with a silver cake basket and knife. But before the spokesman would hand over the knife he demanded a penny from the bride to offset ill-luck. This she smilingly produced and the recipient said he would have it engraved and keep it as a memento. Dutch brides received wafer irons with the bridegroom's coat of arms, initials and the wedding date;

English brides brass warming-pans, inscribed 'Love and Live in Peace'; Austrian girls, painted wooden tubs enjoining 'Be Happy and Industrious'. The tub would carry small possessions to the new home. A girl marrying a Yorkshire farmer expected a bright new 'butter penny' which, laid on the scale with the 'pundstan', a natural stone weighing exactly one pound, ensured that no customer at the farm dairy could complain of short weight.

Traditional gifts such as these survived until relatively recent years. When about 1910 a Herefordshire blacksmith's daughter married, she wore a 'gown', held a reception in a marquee, and left for the honeymoon by car. It could have been a society wedding, but for one touch: the bridegroom's father gave the couple a *pig*. The bride afterwards commended the pig as by far the most valuable of their wedding presents; within a year it had produced no fewer than twenty-eight piglets. In modern Japan, the groom's family at the *yūino*, or betrothal party, gives the bride her wedding kimono embroidered with the groom's crest, and in addition a dress kimono, silk, shoes, hair ornaments, *sake* and fish, and receives a banquet in return. Everything must be in even numbers; two measures of tea, two pairs of toe thongs, two fish: her family reciprocates precisely the groom's gifts and even the basket which carried the groom's fish is packed with the bride's fish for the return journey.

A century ago Finnish brides collected their own wedding gifts, armed with a pillowcase and escorted by an old married man with tophat and umbrella symbolising his 'sheltering' role. Each household gave the faithful follower a drop to help him in his onerous task and by evening his appearance was tragi-comic in the extreme. To omit this bridal-collecting was considered snobbish.

Wedding presents have reflected varied needs. Alice Roosevelt's White House gifts in 1906 included a $1,500 Boston terrier with a complete wardrobe of suits, shoes, furs and petticoats and its regimen engraved upon a silver plate. But when Jairus A. Potter, carpenter, married Elizabeth Allen, maid of all work, at the Pack Log Tavern, Madison, Wisconsin, in April 1838 'the presents were not costly nor numerous, but they were unique and useful to a young family in a new country . . .

milking stool, empty champagne basket with rockers . . . fish-hook and line . . . '.[14]

At the American ritual of the 'bridal shower' – sometimes specifically a 'kitchen shower' (pots, pans, cooking implements), a 'bar shower' (glasses, coasters, cocktail shakers), a 'closet shower' (shoe trees and brushes, coat-hangers and garment-bags) – friends present the bride with small gifts. A popular bride receives several showers, usually following luncheon or bridge parties in her honour. In theory, at least, the gifts surprise her. The bridegroom may receive a 'honey do' shower in anticipation of his future household duties ('honey, do this, honey, do that'), with gifts of aprons, dustpans, brushes and other useful tools.

At the 'trousseau tea', about a week before the wedding, the bride's slips, panties and nightdresses are displayed. It is, of course, unlucky to show the wedding-dress itself and every garment must have been tried on before showing: one girl, about to display her pink wedding slippers just arrived by mail, was saved by a concerted outcry from her family, who shuddered at calamity so nearly averted. The wedding presents, perhaps specially arranged on white satin-covered tables by decorators from a local store, are similarly shown to admiring friends and neighbours, but the value of modern gifts has created new problems. Brought to a recent shower at Bridgeport, Connecticut, were a king-sized bed, two vacuum cleaners and three colour television sets; today it is not unusual for an armed security guard to stand over the treasures. Such exhibitions are far from new: in Turkey a century ago, trousseau items, furred under-garments, linens and prayer carpet, were hung on cords along the walls of the bridegroom's house; furniture was shown in another room and garlands of artificial flowers dressed the 'bride's corner' where her jewellery glittered under glass.

A solemn passage rite moved the bride's goods to her new home. In rural Germany she must arrange her spinning wheel in the dowry cart with distaff facing the house, or she would die in childbirth; she must weep bitterly as she followed the cart, or marriage would be tearful. In the Black Forest a handheld crucifix offset 'crosses' later and the bridegroom sprinkled the goods with holy water and crossed them with consecrated chalk for extra safety. Among Scottish fisher folk it was unlucky for the 'kist' or bride's chest to be moved on a Friday, the day of the crucifixion, ill-omened for new enterprises of any kind, from marriage to sowing a field or killing a pig. The bride locked her kist, the best man laid the key over his heart and the procession moved off to the bridegroom's house. There the kist was set upon the doorstep and unlocked by the bride, who lifted its lid three times to an incantation marking her entry into married life. Chinese brides passed their clothes ceremonially over a purifying, fertilizing fire, before sending them to the bridegroom's home.

In Italy in 1880 the bride's friends transported her property: the more the goods the greater the envy. The contents of each drawer, removed from its chest, were meticulously arranged to stand public inspection which they would certainly receive. One girl carried the pillow, another the looking-glass; behind came the donkey with the mattress. In Normandy everything was crammed on to a decorated waggon; on top was hoisted the finely carved chest or *babut*, central ornament of the new home. The seamstress of the linen rode on the cart, handing pins to any single girls the procession met, wishing them speedy marriage.

CALLING THE BANNS

Banns, public announcements of marriage intention, marked a commitment only slightly less binding than matrimony itself. Those who changed their minds afterwards 'mocked the church' and might be fined. They certainly suffered disapproval in the community. No bride (or in Italy bridegroom) should hear banns called, or her children will be born deaf and dumb. Banns must never be called partly in one year and partly in another: ('straddling the quarters' was almost as ill-advised). Prudent couples still arrange that banns be called at the waxing moon.

The English Marriage Act of 1753 required the public calling of banns unless a special licence were obtained and while this curbed irregularities it roused the obloquy of critics; Horace Walpole wrote to a friend on 22 May:

It is well you are married! How would my lady Ailesbury have liked to be asked in the parish church for three Sundays running! I really believe she would have worn her weeds for ever rather than have passed through so impudent a ceremony!

In New York too, banns were only for the vulgar, special licences genteel, until retrenchments provoked by the Stamp Act forced a change of mind. A newspaper report of 13 December 1765 referred to the aversion thus:

We are creditably informed that there was married last Sunday evening, by the Rev. Mr. Auchmuty, a very respectable couple that had published three different times in Trinity Church. A laudable example and worthy to be followed. If this decent, and for many reasons, proper, method of publication, was once generally to take place, we should have no more of clandestine marriage; and save the expense of licences, no inconsiderable sum these hard and depressing times!

SMOCK WEDDINGS

It was widely believed until the last century that a husband could not be held liable for his wife's debts if she were married barefoot and clad only in shift or smock. Since he acquired an absolute interest in his wife's personal estate, said amateur lawyers, if she brought neither clothes nor property with her, creditors were hamstrung. Brides might strip to their shifts within the church door: but the *Chester Courant*, 24 June 1800, reported a bolder performer who 'went as a bride like Mother Eve to the altar'. This was too much. The clergyman jibbed and refused to perform the ceremony, although usually parsons, if startled, found nothing in the rubric to forbid such lack of clothing. In pioneer New England a creditor might follow a bride no further if she married 'in her shift on the king's highway'. When a smock wedding was performed in the snow at York, Maine, in February 1774, the minister gallantly threw his coat over the shivering bride; in 1789 at Newfane, Vermont, Widow Hannah Ward stood naked in a closet and through a diamond-shaped hole in the door held out her hand to marry Major Moses Joy, who thoughtfully stowed Mrs Ward's bridal finery in the closet beforehand, so that she might emerge resplendent after the ceremony.

The last recorded smock wedding – showing another twist of the ritual was at Halifax, Nova Scotia, where in 1874 a clergyman called to a house to find the woman in a smock, muffled in a shawl, sitting upon a sofa; she told him 'I am a widow, sir, and wish to be married again, but as my first husband died in debt, I wish to be married in my shift, so as not to be responsible for his debts.'[15]

FLEET MARRIAGES, GRETNA GREEN
AND OTHER IRREGULARITIES

The Marriage Act of 1753 ended the London scandal of Fleet marriages. Such illicit, speedy ceremonies had apparently originated with the incumbents of Trinity Minories and St James's, Duke's Place, who claimed immunity from the Bishop of London's jurisdiction. In 1616 the practice was adopted by the fraternity of clerical prisoners within the Fleet debtors' prison, who with neither cash, character nor liberty gladly profited by marrying couples without asking awkward questions. Eighty-three Fleet parsons are known by name: one, rotund and cheerful, was called 'The Bishop of Hell'.

The intoxicated, abducted and unwilling were hurried to the Fleet chapels and to their rivals, the Mayfair, Mint and Savoy; fortune hunters, ladies with debts, spinsters pursuing husbands, paupers and peers; notables such as Lord Abergavenny, Viscount Sligo and Henry Fox, Lord Holland. An impatient Duke of Hamilton wedded the youngest of the beautiful Gunning sisters in the Mayfair chapel at half-past midnight, with a ring torn from the bedcurtains. When the navy was in port it was nothing for 300 sailors to seek the parsons' services. 'Walk in and be married,' shouted the touts outside the 'marriage houses' or 'chapels' round the Fleet. When Richard Leaver was tried for bigamy in 1737 he denied all knowledge of the woman claiming to be his wife. After a drunken evening he had awakened to find himself in bed with a stranger; 'Who are you?' demanded Mr Leaver. 'My dear, we were married last night at the Fleet,' was the reply.

A Fleet parson greets a bridal couple at the 'marriage chapel': the print, 'A Fleet Wedding', engraved by J. Jume, was published 20 October 1747. In the background is the Fleet Market, Farringdon Street: appropriately the street vendor is selling rue

All efforts to halt the abuse failed while such marriages remained legal, but Lord Hardwicke's Act made the solemnisation of marriages without banns or licence, church or chapel, a transportable felony. The parsons went down fighting. The Rev Alexander Keith's marriage business flourished until his prosecution and excommunication in 1742; in retaliation he promptly excommunicated the Bishop of London and the judge of the ecclesiastical court. In 1743 he was committed to the Fleet – for, it was said, contempt of the church – and quickly resumed his old trade; as a last fling on the day before the Act came into effect, he married sixty-one couples and, vowing eternal vengeance on bishops, bought several acres of land for burials, threatening to underbury them all.

As Fleet marriages died, those at Gretna Green sprang to life. Thomas Pennant in his *Tour in Scotland*, 1774–5, suggested:

> . . . stop at the little village of Gretna, the resort of all amorous couples whose union the prudence of parents or guardians

prohibits. Here the young pair may be instantly united by a fisherman, a joiner, or a blacksmith, who may marry for a fee from two guineas a job, to a dram of whiskey. . . . the high priest . . . appears in the form of a fisherman, a stout fellow in a blue coat, rolling round his solemn chaps a quid of tobacco of no common size.

Gretna, in Dumfriesshire, about 9 miles from the border of England and Scotland was first halting-place for runaway couples fleeing from parental wrath and English law with its tiresome requirements of parents' consent to the marriage of minors, of priest and banns. Scottish marriage law required merely a declaration before witnesses: instant marriage. Many cashed in on the business; George Gordon, an old soldier, officiated at weddings in full but ancient military rig; Joseph Paisley, fisherman, smuggler and tobacconist, was also prominent. *The Gretna Green Memoirs* asserted, creditably or otherwise, that 7,744 persons were married by one 'priest' alone between 1811 and 1839. The postboys were heavily involved and received half the fees of perhaps 100 guineas from wealthy clients. When the Earl of Westmoreland eloped with Miss Child, the bank heiress, the couple were pursued by the bride's enraged father, who almost caught them at the border. But the earl drew his pistol, shot Mr Child's leading horse and the lovers reached Gretna safely.

In the eighteenth century Parson Flagg's home at Chester, Vermont, was called the 'Yankee Gretna Green'. To increase revenues the government issued marriage licences at two guineas each, which easy-going parsons like Flagg kept on hand for immediate use at higher prices. 'Flagg marriages' dispensed with the delay of 'publishing'. One girl, about to be married to a man not of her choosing, waited until her party set out to meet the bridegroom, then, with a sympathiser, galloped off pillion to marry her sweetheart Flagg style.

Under pioneer conditions the bridegroom might enjoy unusual experiences. Joseph Hill, justice of the peace for Walworth County, Wisconsin, and Lydia M. Warren of Hubbard, were to be married by Barnabas Snow, on 26 January 1846. But Mr Snow found himself stormbound 13 miles away. A guest pointed out helpfully that, ex officio, the bridegroom could perform the marriage ceremony himself – and he wasted no time in doing so.

On a Louisiana plantation near Natchez in the mid-nineteenth century, bridegroom and best man stood ready in the parlour: the bride entered. But the minister examining the licence exclaimed in horror: 'It is for a wedding in Mississippi and here we are in Louisiana!' Consternation reigned until the plantation owner suggested that the whole bridal party be rowed over to the opposite bank of the river, where the young couple were married on a sandbar. As the minister held up his hand in blessing the plantation bell rang out across the water and a cheer went up from the negroes assembled on the opposite bank.[16] This choice of marriage setting was ordained by fate, but in recent years other couples deliberately seeking the unconventional, have been married in balloons, on water skis, in Forest Lawn cemetery, California. At Corpus Christi, Texas, a 'topless' dancer was married during the floor show, in a white veil and a traditional white wedding gown *sans* front. The bridesmaid was in topless blue. In 1973 a Toronto couple decided to get married on a moving streetcar (which the Toronto Transit Commission renamed 'Devotion' for the occasion) and the bridegroom, minister, bride and sixty guests all boarded at different stops.

In early eighteenth-century New England 'disorderly marriages' (usually of Quakers) were fined until regularised. One stubborn Quaker in New London, Connecticut, declared his intention of taking a wife minus a ceremony of which he could not approve. The scandal was great. But a pious magistrate, meeting the pair in the street and addressing himself to the problem, stopped to ask the Quaker if he persisted in calling this woman, who was a servant and younger than he, his wife? 'Yes, I do!,' said John Rogers stoutly. 'And do you, Mary, wish such an old man as this to be your husband?' 'Indeed I do'. 'Then,' said the governor, coldly but triumphantly, 'by the laws of God and of this commonwealth, I, as magistrate, pronounce you man and wife!' 'Ah, Gurdon, Gurdon', said the bridegroom, with wan admiration, married in spite of himself, 'thee's a cunning fellow'.

Gypsy couples in Europe marry by 'leaping the broomstick' –

a branch of green broom, bearing sweet-scented yellow flowers to benefit the couple's fertility. If the woman's skirt touched the branch, it shows that she has lost her virginity or is pregnant on the wedding day; if the man's trousers touch the broom he will prove unfaithful. Both leap high.

THE WEDDING EVE

From Switzerland to Scotland and Assam the passage rite of bathing bride and groom is performed on the wedding eve. Particularly significant is the bathing of feet which will carry the couple into their new lives. Of Fifeshire a hundred years ago an observer wrote:

> A tub of water was placed in the best room and the bride's feet washed by her female friends — the men, standing outside the door, making jokes and endeavouring to catch a glimpse of the operations. As soon as this washing was finished the bridegroom was brought in and amidst much merriment, made to sit at the tub; his stockings were then pulled off, his legs grasped in any but a gentle manner, and unsparingly daubed by all who get near with a mixture of grease, soot, ashes, and a few cinders. There was great struggling to avoid this part of the performance; however it did not slacken the energies of the company and lucky was the man who escaped with only slight scratches . . .

Many a Scottish bridegroom good humouredly endures feetwashing today. In Java the bride herself washes her husband-to-be's feet; Persian brides and grooms wash each other's big toes before entering the new home and Jewish brides attend the *mikvah* or ritual bath. In another passage rite a Japanese bride burned all the toys and playthings of her childhood and accepted a distaff and flax in exchange.

Evil spirits are believed to be intensely vigilant on the wedding eve. Racket deters them and crockery-breaking accompanies pre-wedding feasts. Lord Malmesbury, marrying a Prussian princess in 1791 as proxy for the Duke of York, heard with amazement that on the morning after the wedding a hundredweight of sherds had been cleared from the princess' door. In the Rhineland, as the wedding-eve party ended, every piece of cracked crockery in the house was hurled from bedroom windows; neighbours dismissed the din with indulgent smiles and 'It's only Fraulein Schmidt's *polterabend*!'. Similar customs were observed in Switzerland. In the Middle East music and dancing enliven houses of both bride and bridegroom; neither sleeps lest the spirits strike. The bridegroom's 'stag party' on the wedding eve, with singing, drinking and, after the bride's health has been drunk, breaking glasses, has similar protective intention. There may be other amusements: police in Leicester, England, reported in 1972 that they had to use a hammer and chisel to free a man who staggered into the police station wearing a steel chastity belt. He said that friends had clamped the belt on him and locked it, at the party on the night before his wedding.

4

THE WEDDING DAY – 1

CHOOSING THE DAY

'Marry in May, rue for aye' is an old saying and May weddings are still often avoided. The Rev Alfred Gatty wrote from Ecclesfield, Yorkshire, England, on 29 April 1850, that a colonial bishop and an archdeacon were both officiating at weddings in his church that day, at the request of brides who flatly refused to be married in May. Queen Victoria told the Princess Royal in 1867 that on no account would she allow any of her children to marry in May and when on 15 May 1567, Mary, Queen of Scots, married the Earl of Bothwell, the line from Ovid:

> Mense malum Maio nubere vulgus ait
> (Common folk say 'tis ill to wed in May)

was found affixed to the gates of Holyrood House, Edinburgh, on the following morning.[17]

The prohibition is perhaps connected with the Roman May festivals of *Bona Dea*, goddess of chastity, and the *lemuralia*, feast of the dead, events which marked May as unpropitious for living marriage. Plutarch certainly offered this explanation; but the belief was old when he wrote. Perhaps the true roots lie in the Celtic tradition, when May, start of summer, was dedicated to extra-marital outdoor lovemaking. The sun shone, the cuckoo called ('Cuckoo, cuckoo, – O word of fear, Unpleasing to the married ear,' wrote Shakespeare, familiar with the age-old connection of cuckoos with deceived husbands). Husbands were mocked in May, thoughts erotic and far from domestic duties:

> Sweep the house with blossomed broom in May
> And you'll sweep the head of the house away.

Housework should be set aside before the pleasures of the month; in Devon and in rural France, May laundry is still avoided; May-born cats (creatures of the domestic hearth) are indifferent mousers and bring snakes into the house; May-born babies languish. The moral is plain enough: it is an ill-omened month indeed to begin domestic life. Agricultural communities also understandably discouraged the disruption of weddings at times of heavy fieldwork. In the Swiss Alps weddings must be over before hayharvest and 'never marry during harvest or you'll have no rest from worries and work,' said the Irish. 'They that wive between sickle and scythe, shall never thrive'. The modern liking for June weddings developed when most people were no longer concerned with agriculture; but many farmers still marry with an eye to the calendar.

So summer was the time for lovemaking and work, the dark months for marriages. In Japanese villages the tenth, eleventh and twelfth lunar months are still favoured; in the Shetland Isles, Hallowe'en was correct for marriage divination, winter for weddings; in Ireland, Christmas to Lent was matchmaking time and at Shrovetide the still unmarried were cruelly mocked, dragged through the streets in derision or sarcastically recommended (even within living memory) to visit the Skelligs Islands where the old calendar was observed to a late date, allowing marriages to take place after Lent had begun on the mainland. Autumn and winter were everywhere dedicated to home life, households and husbands; granaries were full and lonely bachelors' thoughts turned towards domestic comforts. An old verse expresses the benefits of such arrangements:

> Marry in September's shine,
> Your living will be rich and fine.
> If in October you do marry,
> Love will come but riches tarry.
> If you wed in bleak November,
> Only joy will come remember.
> When December's showers fall fast,
> Marry and true love will last.

In old China the time of the first new moon of the year or the season of the first peach blossom were favoured for weddings; similarly in Scotland and Ireland a symbolic fresh start was awaited:

> Marry when the year is new,
> Always loving, always true.

One man, marrying on 31 December, remarked with rare candour that he merely intended to give the lie to the saying that 'you always repent of marriage before the year is out'. In Lincolnshire, England, 21 December, shortest day of the year, was favoured as 'leaving less time for repentance' but Childermass, 28 December, Holy Innocents' Day (so unlucky that even the day of the week upon which it fell was tainted for that year) was universally shunned. In the rural USA young people are urged to marry in the sign of Scorpio, which rules the loins; no consideration matters more. In fourteenth and fifteenth century diagrams of 'zodiacal man', the scorpion, the eighth sign, entered by the sun about 23 October, always over-laid the genitals.

In ancient Greece winter marriages at full moon were favourable; in Rome those at the waxing moons of late autumn. Confidence in the moon's fertilizing influence is worldwide. Country people in Cambridgeshire regard the September harvest moon as the best time for weddings. No German peasant would contemplate marriage at any other time and 'tom cattin' ' is always most satisfactory then, say Ozarks mountain boys; a man is safe from venereal infections and will be refreshed, rather than exhausted by his exploits. It is folly to embark upon lovemaking, let alone matrimony, in the wane. In Holland and along the eastern coast of Scotland, the tide must be rising during the marriage ceremony, magically expressing the inflowing of riches and children to the couple.

The early Church had prohibited marriages during Lent, Whitsun or Advent. (In the Eastern Orthodox Church full weddings, with reception, are still forbidden during Lent, although in emergencies, such as time of war, a simple ceremony is permitted.) The church register of St Mary's, Beverley, Yorkshire, contains these explanatory lines written in

1641 by the Rev Nicholas Osgodby:

> When Advent comes do thou refraine,
> Till Hillary sett ye free againe;
> Next Septuagesima saith thee nay;
> But when Low Sunday comes thou may;
> Yet at Rogation thou must tarrie,
> Till Trinitie shall bid thee marry.

Today Lent marriages are still sometimes felt to be unsuitable, even by those whose religious convictions are vague. The belief has proved durable: 'Marry in Lent, live to repent' is the discouraging prediction.

Days of the week were important also. In Italy, Sunday was the day for weddings; a couple married on Monday would have girls or idiots among their children; Tuesday's first boy would be a fawn, or clubfooted; Thursday was the day of witches; Wednesday and Friday, fast days. A widely quoted rhyme influenced others:

> Monday for wealth,
> Tuesday for health,
> Wednesday best day of all,
> Thursday for losses,
> Friday for crosses,
> And Saturday, no luck at all.

In New England there was never a marrying on ill-omened Friday, 'hangman's day'.

In old China, fortune-tellers determined a suitable day for the 'red affair': red represented wedding happiness: a red sedan chair fetched the bride, clad in red dress and headdress: red was the only colour for wedding umbrellas, tapers, gift boxes – even betrothal letters were written upon red paper. The immutability of a propitious wedding day can change lives. In 1974 the nationwide railway strike in India involving over one million railway workers and 10,000 long-distance trains, meant that as many as 200,000 Hindu couples and their families could not meet for weddings on appointed days. Hindu 'alliances' are arranged by parents after prolonged negotiation and the exact date and time of the wedding is fixed by family priests and astrologers after examination of the couple's horoscopes. If the appointed hour is missed a wait of perhaps a year for another as auspicious may be necessary. A teacher at a Bombay high school was to marry a chemical engineer in Calcutta: during the strike the bridegroom's party, in a fleet of hired taxis, raced 1,500 miles in three days to the rendezvous, but arrived at the Bombay marriage hall two hours after the appointed time. The astrologers quickly conferred, pronouncing the next suitable day as in February 1975, and to mollify the bridegroom's parents the bride's family promptly increased her dowry of $7,600. Some marriages were cancelled completely after such setbacks – to the satisfaction of a few brides who had not cared for their parents' choice of mate; to them George Fernandos, the strikers' leader, was a hero.[18]

Many weddings still take place at Easter when Lent ends. Sir George Head in *A Home Tour Through the Manufacturing Districts of England*, 1835, wrote of Easter weddings in Manchester parish church to which weddingers were attracted by low fees. Banns had been called for 197 couples; Sir George arrived at the church at 8 am and marrying began at 10. At first the congregation was silent and subdued but high spirits soon asserted themselves and jokes flew back and forth; a shy bridegroom was greeted with an encouraging shout of 'Come in, man! What art thou afraid of? Nobody'll hurt thee!' and general laughter all round.

The clerk soon had the bridal couples and their friends marshalled round the altar. In his friendly Lancashire way he set everyone at ease: 'Daniel and Phoebe; this way, Daniel, take off your gloves, Daniel. William and Anne; no Anne, here Anne; t'other side, William . . . now all of you give your hats to some person to hold . . . '. Although the service was addressed to all, the clergyman scrupulously obtained responses from each person; a wise precaution, for on one legendary occasion, on a busy day, the Rev Joshua Brookes had accidentally married the wrong parties to each other. When the error was pointed out he brushed the difficulty aside with a brisk 'Pair as you go out! You're all married, pair as you go out!'

But similar confusion might have more lasting and damaging

results. Among the Armenians there were lucky days for marriage and many couples presented themselves at church on the same favoured day. On one occasion at Broussa in the late nineteenth century, confusion was great; brides, dressed alike and blindfolded by heavy enveloping crimson veils, were pushed forward by a dense crowd of relatives and friends; two of like stature accidentally changed places. One was a pretty peasant girl, promised bride of a blacksmith, the other the plain daughter of a wealthy city burgher, whose bridegroom was of like class. Not until the end of the ceremony was the disastrous mistake discovered. There was no remedy, so all parties wisely agreed to make the best of a bad job and to 'accept the partners whom Fate had unexpectedly assigned them'.[19]

The idea of marriages en masse survives with vigour at Las Vegas, Nevada, where couples marry at the courthouse or at one of the many wedding chapels – ('No Waiting. Open 24 Hours a Day. Major Credit Cards Accepted') – with such names as Cupid's Wedding Chapel, Chapel of the Roses, Desert Bells Chapel, Little Chapel Around the Corner or The Hitching Post. On busy days licensed ministers – 'Marryin' Sams' – perform ceremonies every fifteen minutes for hours on end.

Such arrangements cannot please everyone. In Prospect Park, Brooklyn, New York, in 1967, nine young couples (of the fifty invited) were married by a magistrate in the city's first municipally-sponsored 'wed-in'. Trousseaux, rings, seven-tier wedding cakes, paper dresses for bridesmaids, bouquets and honeymoons were provided by local enterprises at a cost of about $2,000 for each couple. Staider citizens were shocked; the chief city clerk is reported to have condemned the wed-in as 'an offensive common spectacle' and to have suggested that the parks department had erred in taste in organizing the event. A complete review of judges' privileges to perform marriages was immediately put in hand by the city clerk's department which controls such matters.[20]

WEDDING-DAY WEATHER

It is a worldwide belief that life-giving sunshine benefits brides. 'Happy the bride the sun shines on' is expressed in many languages. A Parsee bride looks towards the sun as she is dressed on her wedding morning; in the Scottish Highlands the bride walked 'with the sun' from east to west on the south side of the church which she circled three times sunwise to honour the source of all life. To neglect this ritual invited calamity. The Chaco Indians of South America do not consider any marriage to be ratified until the sun has shone upon the feet of the newlyweds the next morning. A solar eclipse on the wedding day naturally suggests darkening fortunes to come. The sun is widely regarded as a powerful stimulant to sex, hence the belief that those of the Latin and negro races, from hot countries, are more virile and passionate than the fair-skinned. The modern liking by men for a suntan and the general use of sunlamps (also said to stimulate the male sexual drive) are other contemporary expressions of this old superstition.

Wedding-day snow, symbolically suggesting a rain of riches (or perhaps troubles so light as to be barely perceptible) is fortunate; the Japanese believe that it is particularly lucky for the bride to carry flowers plucked in snow by a maiden friend. Rain on the day not surprisingly signifies tears ahead; although in Sweden rain falling on the bridal wreath is seen as a beneficent anointing. A thunderstorm during the marriage service condemns the couple to childlessness.

Across America the wedding day is the 'bride's day' and its weather, hour by hour, reflects the coming pattern of her life. A fine morning and a stormy afternoon portend a tranquil beginning but difficulties later. The following day is the groom's, with portents for him, and the third day, belonging to the pair together, reveals their future life — sunny and placid, lowering and quarrelsome.

GOOD LUCK AND ILL: TAKING PRECAUTIONS

Outdoor omens had greater force before nineteenth-century affluence and the coming of bridal carriages and cars for all. Earlier, on a slower journey, as the bridal party had walked or ridden on horseback to church, it had been tempting to look about for signs of coming luck or woe. It is a fortunate bride who, in America, Canada, Belgium, Spain and some other

European countries, meets a white cat; in England a black cat. A funeral or a pig in the path of a Scottish bridal party was enough to turn it round to make a fresh start. The sad sight of a cripple, suggesting deformed children for the couple, or a monk or nun, symbolising enforced chastity and barrenness, was ill, but the European gipsy bride welcomed the sight of woman of easy virtue – the easier the better – for it promised cheerful abundance. Although ever harder to achieve with fewer open fires, it is lucky for a bride to meet a chimney-sweep with blackened face, sootladen brushes and magical associations with the family hearth, heart of the house. This meeting was often contrived by the best man, who bribed the sweep, with a shilling and a glass of beer, to kiss the bride. A dark skin has protective connotations also which added to the value of the encounter: a Nigerian law student, Sam Ekpenyon, an air-raid warden during the London bombings of 1941, found that some shelterers thought him so lucky that they would not settle down for the night until he had visited them.

To distract the malevolent it was wise to use alternative routes to and from church and there must be no separation of bride and groom on the way, lest it precede real separation later. No cat or dog must run between the pair and in Armenia no person was permitted to pass between the bride's and the bridegroom's processions. In Wales and Switzerland the couple walked pressed closely together to prevent demons from casting malignant shadows between them, and kept eyes cast modestly downwards, lest either be tempted to glance at another. Ahead of the Persian procession and before the Chinese bride's sedan chair, walked a man bearing a mirror whose reflection would divert the evil eye from the bride and Swedish brides wore bells and sparkling trinkets upon their wedding costumes to deflect evil, just as gleaming brasses protect a team of horses from witchcraft.

Many were the charms against witches and fairies who eyed the bridal party. In Sweden the bridegroom sewed sprigs of garlic, thyme and other strongly-scented plants into his clothing, and bridesmaids carried posies of herbs. In south Arabia the bridegroom wears garlic in his turban: and in Palestine the time-honoured prophylactic, salt, is tossed over the heads of the wedding party. Mothers of German brides dropped dill and salt into their daughters' wedding shoes, to the protective charm:

> Dill cease not from will, salt relax not . . .

and in Russia the doors, windows and chimney of the wedding house, where a witch might enter, were carefully sealed.

In Syria the bridal procession never passes a cemetery (for obvious reasons) or, more subtly, a baker's shop, lest the bride develop a gluttonous appetite for sweet pastries. Brides once disliked marrying with a grave standing open in the churchyard or on a day when the passing bell was rung at the death of a married woman; no bride entered church through the door used by funeral processions. It was ill-luck if the church clock struck during the marriage service and prudent bridal parties waited until the quarter before moving briskly inside, to secure the maximum safe period within.

In Germany one of the pair would die within a year if the priest sneezed during the wedding ceremony (perhaps because the sneeze was believed to be an early symptom of dreaded plague). In Alabama whichever of the pair rose first from the altar would be first to die and in Belgium (less ominously) would be first to rise in the household each morning. A Yorkshire bride was warned by her maid to make her responses quietly: 'Why, ma'am, you know them 'at speaks loudest dies first.'

It is still felt to be dangerous for a bride to count her chickens before they are hatched. Girls frequently refuse to read the wedding service beforehand and seek proxies for wedding rehearsals. Trousseaux are rarely fully assembled before the wedding eve, and linen is still marked with the bride's maiden rather than married initials. A wise girl does not practise signing her new name until it is hers. And of course no one must address her by it in advance. In the early days of photography, a mysterious art, engaged couples were uneasy about being photographed together, lest they seem to anticipate the married state.

A bride weeps on her wedding day, or tears will fall later.

Moroccan bridesmaids pinch a too cheerful bride to induce tears – and copious rain for crops. In the Austrian Tyrol a tearful bride received from her mother a finely embroidered handkerchief, not to be used again until it covered her face at death. The idea of the bridal handkerchief (even if not intended for a flood of tears), survives: when President Grant's daughter Nellie married from the White House in 1874, she received a $500 lace handkerchief for her trousseau, and when a young Canadian bride, Martha J. Rogers, married James A. Kellam in Vancouver in 1973 she carried in her bouquet two antique handkerchiefs – one of lace, the other tatted.

A bridal couple, hoping for fertility for themselves, had the power to bestow it on others. In Norway and Sweden, to promote a good crop of calves the newlyweds visited the cowshed on their return from church, and in full bridal finery the bride took care to milk a cow, to ensure that her household would never lack milk. Friends of Bohemian brides hid feathers and flaxseed in their shoes, to make certain of an abundance of feather beds and linen for the couple in years to come. An acorn in the bridegroom's pocket gave him long life and the sturdy qualities of the oak tree. German brides carried in their shoes a hair from every single animal on the farm, and the bridegroom a sample of every kind of grain from the fields, to stimulate the farm's fertility. In Morocco the bride's *baraka* or blessing is transferable to grain lying in her lap while she is dressed and this, with her hair combings, is thrown into a furrow at planting time, to ensure bountiful crops. Everything associated with weddings brings luck: even the old-fashioned cottage-window plant, *Francoa ramosa*, the 'bridal wreath', spread happiness from its place on the window-sill.

Until recent years household bees were often told the family's news; and if this duty were neglected they might die or fly away. On wedding days white ribbons fluttered from their straw hives to honour the bride and one family remembered with pleasure that with them a bee had actually gone to church clinging to the bride's bouquet – a happy omen indeed. Swarming on the wedding day was full of promise of future increase. In Normandy bees were said to waste no time in stinging a girl who had anticipated the pleasure of marriage.

For a younger sister or brother to marry before the elder demolished proper order and provoked ill-luck. As an antidote the elder child must dance bare-foot in the hogtrough on the wedding day. About 1860 one Suffolk bride's brother performed with such abandon that the trough fell to pieces; when about 1880 a servant girl in Shropshire, England, refused to dance thus, her aunt scolded her next day saying 'So I hear you didna dance barfut! I'm ashamed of you ... I've a good mind to pull off yer boots for ye now this minute and make ye dance i' the street!'

Luck-bringing shoe customs are found at weddings the world over. When Queen Alexandra's protégée, Doris Vivian, married from Buckingham Palace, as she and the groom, Douglas Haig, were about to drive away, someone ran forward to tie an old shoe to their carriage in time-honoured tradition. 'No, No!,' cried the queen. 'They must have this one' and hopped forward holding out her own silk slipper. In a double charm at a Scottish border wedding in 1879 a pair of *baby* shoes was tied to the bridal carriage. Shoe lore is constantly updated: when the cross-Channel British Rail hovercraft *Princess Anne* left Dover for Calais on the princess's wedding morning of 14 November 1973, she trailed two old boots behind her.

Shoes are closely associated with their owners' life essence and have been found hidden in walls of old houses, apparently as protective charms: their wedding importance may be a related belief. Shoes are often thrown after the pair for luck. Some say this recalls the bride-fight when all handy missiles were snatched up, others that it betokens transference of authority from father to husband. The prevalence of new shoes in wedding lore also suggests a passage rite. In Berri, in central France, the best men, echoing *Cinderella*, attempted to fit the bride's new shoes on her, but all failed except the bridegroom. In Yugoslavia the bride received new shoes after her ceremonial dance at the wedding feast.

Shoe stealing is another unexplained wedding sport. Pakistani wedding guests remove their shoes before the ceremony in the customary way, but find the bridegroom curiously reluctant to part with his, for he knows that they will be hidden and only released after payment of a forfeit. Shoes have played a role in marriage divination. At a Leicestershire wedding about 1868, the bride's brother threw a tramp's boot clean over the bridal carriage into the rhododendrons, and in full bridal gear the bridesmaids plunged after it. One – who would be first to marry – bore it out in triumph, and the boot hung from a beam by a white satin ribbon for the rest of the wedding day, for luck. The custom was well known too in Germany.

Not everyone, of course, wished the couple well. Disappointed suitors and spiteful relatives could be depended upon to harbour wedding day grudges. Rev H. Morland Austen, of St Peter's, Thanet, Kent, wrote on 6 April 1850 that when he had married a couple the previous Saturday, the bridegroom's old aunt, disapproving of the match, turned up to pronounce an impressive malediction on the couple, and returned home to sweep her doorstep ritually with a new broom, to 'sweep her nephew from it forever', and then to hang the broom over her door in final and public rejection.

THE WEDDING DRESS AND CROWN

Lively beliefs surround the wedding dress. Maureen Baker of Susan Small Limited of London, designer of Princess Anne's dress for her wedding in Westminster Abbey to Captain Mark Phillips, spoke of traditions observed in her workroom. Whistling is banned, as it is on a boat, down a mine or in the theatre; the belief is ancient and may be connected with whistling up evil spirits. No tacking with black thread – of funeral associations – is allowed. Fifteen Susan Small workers each sewed a hair into the dress as a good-luck charm, although one whose interpretation causes argument. Some feel that the bride benefits less than the owner of the hair and that the procedure is akin to witchcraft. Hair is an essential ingredient of many spells. In the Ozarks, one girl at least is known to have taken a magnifying glass to her wedding clothes to make certain that no such hair had been inserted and there the connotation is sinister rather than lucky.

The French say that a bride lives the same number of years as there are buttons on her wedding dress. A penny sewn into the seam of the gown brings luck wherever it goes later. The seamstress who inserts the first stitch into a wedding dress will herself be married before the year is out. It is generally said that a bride should not make her own dress; even professional dressmakers often avoid the task. The dress is rarely fully completed before the wedding day lest anticipation invite disaster and it is safest to add the final stitch, bow or ribbon, after a final glance in the mirror, at the very moment the bride leaves for church, thus reducing to a minimum the dangerous interval between appearing as a bride and becoming a wife. If the dress is bought readymade, a belt or another detachable part must be left off during the fittings. A wedding dress spreads a general benison and in May 1962 a correspondent wrote to a weekly periodical in England of a dressmaker who always gave to betting friends the pins she had used in making a wedding dress. They found them useful in selecting (with eyes closed) likely winners of horseraces.

It was once felt to be unlucky to sell, remodel, or dye a wedding dress, lest married happiness be imperilled. Country bridegrooms in the USA are still advised not to be too hasty in changing wedding clothes for working overalls; wedding suits should be kept in view and worn occasionally, for several months after the ceremony, to carry wedding luck forward into married life. In more sentimental days the gown and accessories were preserved for later use; after Queen Victoria's death in 1901 her lace wedding veil was laid over her face. Similar feelings live on and every year thousands of American brides send their dresses to a Los Angeles laboratory for ultrasonic dry-cleaning and 'restoration', which guarantees the dress's life for a century. It is then laid to rest in an airtight casket. When unanticipated death was commonplace, marriage and burial seemed close. In Cambridgeshire, England, after the ceremony, the bride embroidered a cross upon her husband's wedding smock which was kept until his burial. In Sweden the wedding shirt, and in Spain the father-in-law's gift of the bridal nightgown, are similarly preserved. Sometimes the couple gave each other a complete set of grave clothes, proudly displayed with the other wedding presents.

Until the nineteenth century dresses were rarely bought specially for weddings; brides merely appeared in their best

Queen Victoria's wedding dress, 1840 (*The Trustees of the London Museum*)

dresses or, in peasant communities, in national costume. A Flatbush, New York, bride was married about 1750 wearing fawn silk over a light blue damask petticoat; and in delicate complement, the bridegroom's waistcoat was of the same damask. At the Quaker wedding at Bank Meeting of Isaac Collins of Burlington, New Jersey, to Rachel Budd of Philadelphia, the bridegroom wore a coat of peach blossom cloth, lined with white quilted silk, a cocked hat, silk stockings and pumps. The bride's dress was of light blue brocade, her shoes the same with heels as small round as a gold dollar. The outfit was completed by a white satin stomacher, blue cord laces and black hood lined with white silk, an accessory of German origin, as common at 18th-century weddings in Philadelphia as the veil is today. At his wedding about 1825, Devon farmer Barnabas Butter wore 'a new bottle-green, swallow-tailed coat, with bright brass buttons, knee-breeches, and a buff jean waistcoat'; his bride, Betty Kick, 'chose her wedding-gown with regard to use, and blue mousseline de laine, with a black silk spencer, was her Sunday dress for several summers after.'[21]

The colour of the wedding dress is important. Except in Norway a green dress, or green garments in the trousseau, are shunned. Green is a fairy colour, it is said, and therefore unlucky, but a green dress once had a more lusty significance. To say that a girl 'had a green gown' was to imply light morals with a predilection for outdoor lovemaking and a grass-stained gown as a natural outcome. Obviously a green-gowned unvirginal girl was hardly likely to make a satisfactory wife. A comprehensive old rhyme goes into wedding colours thoroughly:

> Married in white, you have chosen all right,
> Married in black, you will wish yourself back,
> Married in red, you wish yourself dead,
> Married in green, ashamed to be seen,
> Married in blue, you will always be true,
> Married in pearl, you will live in a whirl,
> Married in yellow, ashamed of your fellow,
> Married in brown, you will live out of town,
> Married in pink, your fortunes will sink.

The first all-white wedding dress of modern times appears to have been chosen by Anne of Brittany for her marriage to Louis XII. The first American bride to wear white was perhaps Decima Cecilia Shubrich of Charleston, South Carolina, a noted beauty who at the age of nineteen married James H. Heyward. Her picture, painted in 1800, shows a tulle wedding veil and pearl tiara. Today most Western brides choose white wedding dresses and during the last century changes have been few. In 1874 Nellie Grant wore a tulle veil and a white satin wedding dress trimmed with point lace, with orange blossoms in her hair: her bridesmaids, white corded silk covered with white silk illusion, with puffs caught up with flowers. Four carried pink roses, four blue. Thirty-two years later Alice Roosevelt married Nicholas Longworth and wore white satin, point lace and a silver brocade train six yards long. These outfits would be unexceptionable today, so constant are wedding tastes.

The words 'white wedding' have become neatly expressive of all the old traditions of white satin, bridesmaids, flowers, bells and wedding cake. 'Are you having a white wedding?' one girl will ask another soon after the announcement of an engagement. White epitomises purity and also deters the evil eye, a constant danger for young virgins of both sexes. At Orthodox Jewish weddings the bridegroom as well as the bride wears white. Significantly it is thought unsuitable for those making second marriages, either as widows or divorcees. But white is not the only wedding colour: during the Revolution American brides favoured red, the colour of defiance. Islamic brides wear the *gharara*, a tunic and ruffled trousers, in red. (In Islamic countries, by contrast, only widows wear white.) Black is correct in some peasant communities: in Iceland, fifty years ago, it was every woman's ambition to have a wedding dress of black velvet, embroidered with gold and silver thread. Yellow is another wedding colour. A Roman bride wore a yellow hair-net and shoes and in the nineteenth century an obliging bride would wear a yellow garter put in place by a girl-friend, to ensure marriage for the friend within the year. One Boston bride in 1895 went to the altar wearing seven yellow garters pressed upon her by the hopeful. As a yellow garter attracts lovers it was highly improper for a married woman to wear one.

Even the most sophisticated of brides is still likely to observe the old dictum:

> Something old, something new,
> Something borrowed, something blue,

in her wedding outfit, sometimes adding 'and sixpence in her shoe', for to carry a coin at the wedding secures future wealth. In Canada, brides in the Rogers family wear a 'shin-plaster' – a 25-cent bill – in their shoes.[22] North Carolina brides carry a gold dollar and a Swedish bride's father slips a silver coin into her left shoe, her mother gold into the right, so that, by imitative magic, she may never lack luxuries. The blue of the rhyme signifies constancy:

> Those dressed in blue
> Have lovers true.

Dressing for the wedding is a rite of passage and brides usually wear new, unlaundered undergarments, even rejecting used pins, thus emphasising their acceptance of a new life. But it is happiness-inducing to include one item already worn by a happy bride, and married women are flattered to be asked to lend their wedding veils for this purpose. Family traditions reinforce the belief: Elizabeth Randolph married William Berkley at Wilton, Virginia, in 1792, wearing a Mechlin lace veil which has been worn since by six generations of the family's brides. The rules about trying on bridal clothes apply with double force to wedding veils, if the veil is put on before the day the bride may be deserted, have an unhappy marriage, or even die before the wedding. Nor should a bride allow a friend to try on the wedding veil, or the friend may run off with the newly-made husband.

Greek brides carry a lump of sugar within their wedding gloves, to give, by magical means, 'sweetness all their married lives' and the idea is found in England also. When Sir John Rothenstein's daughter Lucy married in Westminster Cathedral, London, in 1959, she carried a sachet of sugar tucked into the bodice of her taffeta dress.

Norwegian bridal crown from Numedal in Buskerūd (*Norsk Folkemuseum*)

Until recent years, particularly in the Scandinavian countries, the bridal crown, so heavy as to be an ordeal to wear (perhaps even reducing the bride to a fainting condition), was an important part of the traditional wedding costume. Crowning typified purity and at early Christian weddings the couple were crowned with garlands of myrtle, after the benediction. In the Eastern Orthodox wedding ceremony bride and bridegroom are still given gold crowns to wear. In some regions, bridal crowns and ornaments were parish property, lent to all, so that brides rich or humble might appear at their best on the wedding day. In Finland in the nineteenth century a visitor noted that the crown, poised on piled-up hair, was ornamented with gold leaf, cut-glass ornaments and looking-glass. 'The more noise and jingling this castle made the better. Above it soared a forest of feathers of all colours': in this instance the crown had lost its early connection with purity and had become another gaudy witch-deterrent device. A guest at a Lapp wedding at Koutokaeino at Christmas 1885, saw a crown of coloured silk, with strings of pearls and silver ornaments; the crown closed with a posy of flowers and silver-gilt leaves, with floating coloured silk ribbons. The bridegroom wore his usual blue summer coat with a broad silver belt and a narrow white silk band passed about his neck, criss-crossing over his breast, its ends nearly reaching the ground.[23]

Lapp bridal couple, 1885

In Finland after the wedding the girls danced round the blindfolded bride who held her crown in her hand:

> It has been! It has gone!
> Never will the bride be a maid more:
> Never will she dance with the crown again,

sang the guests: and the bride reached out and crowned one of the dancing girls, who would thus be next to marry.

A nineteenth-century Norwegian bride, dressed in the 'parish ornaments'

THE WEDDING RING

Although completely absent in some non-European countries the wedding ring has deep significance in the United States, Britain and other countries of Europe, expressing through its circular shape the imperishable covenant of marriage.

Perforated stones also had the power to confirm matrimonial contracts. In eighteenth century Orkney, couples cemented their troth by clasping hands through the Standing Stones of Stennis: the Woden Stones would actually marry those who, vowing fidelity, held hands through them. The couple could conveniently terminate the marriage if they wished by attending a service in a church and leaving by different doors. Marriage contracts were still ratified at the Hole Stone at Doagh, County Antrim, Ireland, as late as 1902.

But generally, of course, it has been customary to symbolise everlasting promise with the wedding ring. Today dates, initials and a sentimental word or two are often engraved within it; at one time whole books were devoted to such posies as:

> Not two but one
> Till life be done

and

> A heart content cannot repent

Another bridegroom, franker than the rest, chose:

> Thou wert not handsome, wise, but rich,
> 'Twas that which did my eyes bewitch.

Ring inscriptions have a long history. The ancient Greeks favoured such words as ZEΣ – 'Mayest thou live' and Jewish 'Mizpah' rings, often decorated with a raised device in the shape of a house, containing perfume or a holy relic, refer to Genesis 31, 49, 'the Lord watch between me and thee . . .'. In Germany in the sixteenth and seventeenth centuries Adam and Eve and the 'tree of temptation' were popular devices: Romans chose two hearts held by a key; Finnish rings bore a shield-shaped bezel covered with small silver rings, each, it was said, representing one cow in the dowry. Crusaders favoured rings holding a relic of the True Cross. Gold Claddagh rings, decorated with a heart clasped by two hands, given by a mother to the first of her daughters to marry, were for generations the

A collection of modern gold wedding rings, 1974 (*Courtesy of Tiffany & Co, New York*)

wedding token of the Irish peasantry; Spanish and Breton counterparts suggest that traders carried the design to Ireland.

Wedding rings are traditionally of plain gold of high carat (pure gold is 24 carat) symbolising the nobility of the union. Recently 'antique', 'rope' and 'bark' effects, in tune with current fashions in design, have been about, but it seems unlikely that marked changes lie ahead for wedding rings: the traditional plain gold band is still extremely popular. In emergencies and hard times cheaper materials have been pressed into service; at more than one wedding the ring of the church door key has found a fresh use, but in nineteenth-century Ireland a gold ring was considered essential for the legality of the contract even among the very poor and a ring was borrowed from a friend or hired for the day from the officiating priest.

The 'double ring ceremony' in which the couple exchange identical rings, symbolising the exchange of vows, is increasingly popular. This European practice apparently spread to North America with returning servicemen after World War II and is now favoured, it is said, by 90 per cent of American couples, to the delight of jewellers. The new form of marriage service introduced by the Church of Wales in 1975 provides for the double ring ritual and rings are exchanged 'in token of love and faithfulness'. Perhaps the most recent expression of such shared jewellery is to be seen in the 'Love Bands. The Ties that Bind You Together'— bangle rings, bracelets and necklets in silver with gold roping (reinforcing the symbolism of the binding tie) which are equally suitable for men or women.

Some, including women's liberationists, who usually decline to wear wedding rings, believe that the ring developed from the shackle once put about the bride to subdue her after capture. Certainly in Pliny's time Roman brides wore iron rings said to have been originally links in a chain and the large nose ring of the Moslem bride still denotes her bondage to her husband. On the continent of Europe the wedding ring is often worn on the right hand; in America and Britain on the third finger of the left hand. *The Manual of Sarum Use*, which defined forms of service acceptable in the diocese of Salisbury, England, from the eleventh century to the Reformation, suggests a reason for this choice of finger:

Then let the Bridegroom put the ring on the thumb of the Bride, saying—In the Name of the Father; (on the first finger) and of the Son; (on the second finger) and of the Holy Ghost; (on the third finger). Amen. And there let him leave it, because in that finger there is a certain vein which reaches to the heart.

So firmly did the Greeks and Romans adhere to this imaginative physiology that for extra efficacy their doctors stirred ointment with the ring finger. In country districts the ring finger is still believed to sooth any stye or wart touched by it and in Spain water in which the wedding ring has been dipped is a therapeutic lotion for sore eyes. In the Carpathian mountains of central Europe the milk of a cow milked through a wedding ring could never be stolen by witches. Wedding rings are also important in divination. In an ancient charm of the East, a European gipsy girl attaches a ring to her forefinger by a hair and hangs the ring within a jug on the rim of which are marked the letters of the alphabet. Letters touched by the swinging ring reveal the names of future lovers. In Yorkshire the 'matrimony cake' containing the hostess's wedding ring, a piece of silver and a button, was a favourite party piece. The finder of the ring would soon marry, of the silver be wealthy, but the finder of the button was doomed to spinsterhood.

A wedding ring must never be bought on a Friday, in accord with the ill reputation of this day. In rural America it is ill-advised to buy a ring through a mail-order catalogue lest it should have absorbed bad luck from others who have tried it on, then returned it. The ring must never be put on before the ceremony (or at any time by anyone but the owner, or the tryer-on will never marry). It is of course most unlucky to drop the ring during the ceremony and whichever of the couple does this will be first to die. Should the ring roll away and come to rest upon a tombstone the omen is dire indeed: if the tombstone is that of a woman the bride will die first, if of a man the bridegroom. While in England the ring is traditionally in the best man's charge until needed, in America a small boy, the 'ring-bearer', carries it on a decorated white-satin cushion. For safety's sake it is tied in place with ribbons, or held by a few loose tacking threads which can easily be broken.

WEDDING FLOWERS

Myrtle is held to be the luckiest flower for a window-box and in Wales is planted on either side of the front door to bring harmony to the household. With its white, sweet-smelling flowers and lustrous dark leaves, fragrant when bruised, redolent of romance and happiness, myrtle preceded orange blossom in the bridal bouquet and many bushes at cottage doors owe their existence to the old country custom of planting a sprig from the bride's bouquet when she returned from church. This planting was always done by a bridesmaid, never by the bride, and the future blooming of the bush portended another wedding. If the sprig did not strike, the planter was destined to become an old maid but myrtle's obliging nature made this depressing outcome unlikely. Myrtle grown from Queen Victoria's wedding bouquet in 1840 furnished the traditional sprig for Princess Anne's wedding bouquet in 1973 as well as the requirement of 'something old'. (For the princess 'something borrowed' was the tiara owned by Queen Elizabeth, the Queen Mother, which had been worn by Queen Elizabeth II, then Princess Elizabeth, at her wedding twenty-six years earlier. Apart from myrtle, the princess's bouquet included fifteen white roses, fifty lilies of the valley, a few white orchids and orange blossoms – all traditional wedding flowers.)

Marigold, green broom and rosemary, gilded and dipped into scented rosewater for added fragrance, were favourite wedding plants in Tudor England. (Rosewater in food or drink, Persian brides say, binds a husband to his wife.) As late as 1700 country bridal beds were decked with rosemary for remembrance. In Gloucestershire until a hundred years ago, bridemaids carried white *Achillea Ptarmica* –'seven years' love'– to bring about this happy state for the bride, and French brides believe that mignonette –'little darling'– in the bouquet will hold a husband's affections. The significantly named 'baby's breath', *Gypsophila paniculata*, with a cloud of tiny white flowers, is a bouquet ingredient with obvious fertility connotations: on a day chosen at random in the summer of 1974 twelve out of sixteen brides in Winnipeg, Canada, included baby's breath in their bouquets. The flowering quince, *Cydonia japonica*, is another well-liked bridal flower, deriving from the ancient Greek belief that a shared quince promotes love between husband and wife. Lily of the valley makes a potent love charm, both before and at the wedding. About 1897, a putty figurine of a man, together with withered rosebuds and lily of the valley, was found in a little-used attic under the roof near the servants' quarters at The Poplars, Hereford, England, probably a love charm hidden by a maidservant. In France, lily of the valley is the traditional lover's gift on 1 May, and today both the flower and the scent, 'muguet', are widely advertised as May Day approaches.

The orange tree, simultaneously bearing golden fruit, sweet-scented white flowers and leaves – typifying fertility through this abundance – is a traditional ingredient in love charms and marriage luck. Saracen brides wore its flowers as a sign of fecundity and crusaders are said to have carried the custom to the West. When Jacqueline Kennedy married Aristotle Onassis in Greece in 1968, the couple danced round the altar and were crowned with orange blossoms in the traditional Greek style. Artificial orange blossoms, although ubiquitous, are a little suspect and must be destroyed within a month of the wedding lest their good luck turn to ill.

White is the colour for most weddings and white-petalled flowers – orange blossoms, roses, violets, camellias, lilac, stephanotis and, above all, *Lilium candidum*, the white or madonna lily, are top wedding favourites. While the use of flowers at weddings is as widespread as ever, bouquet shapes have changed. Mrs Slater, chief florist at Moyses Stevens in London and creator of Princess Anne's bouquet, said of the years since Princess Elizabeth's wedding in 1947: 'Bouquets have changed a lot – they're much smaller now, daintier'. Miss B. D. Hadow of the same firm adds: 'Most bouquets these days are chosen, as far as shape and colour are concerned, to complement the bride's dress . . . if the bride is wearing a period dress she would certainly want a loose Victorian posy, probably in a lace frill with ribbons. If . . . she is wearing a modern style, the bouquet would be designed entirely to enhance the design of the dress. We find that brides very rarely come in to ask for any specific flower, but prefer to describe what they and the

Mr and Mrs Percy Evans, married on 3 June 1924, at Quainton, Buckinghamshire, epitomise 'the happy couple'. Mr Evans wears a boutonnière of lilies of the valley and Mrs Evans carries lilies, both traditional wedding flowers (*Albert Cherry*)

bridesmaids are wearing and to ask for our advice as to toning colours, suitable flowers, and overall shape.' American florists report that the once-popular 'arm' and 'shower' bouquets (the latter with tiny flowers attached to satin ribbons falling from the main bouquet) have been eclipsed by bouquets carried in front, such as the 'cascade'– triangular and falling to a slender point. Bouquets are normally the concern of the bride and bridesmaids alone – but in a novel departure at his White House wedding to Nellie Grant, Algernon Sartoris, the *bridegroom*, carried the bouquet of orange blossoms, pink rosebuds and tuberoses, with a trailing streamer inscribed 'LOVE'.[24]

At Western weddings the bridegroom, best man and ushers usually wear white carnations, gardenias or camellias as boutonnières (an American bridegroom in a white wedding jacket, on the other hand, wears a red flower) and by an old tradition the bridegroom is supposed to choose a flower which also appears in his bride's bouquet.

An indispensable American wedding custom, deriving from the old English 'flinging the stocking' (described later) is 'throwing the bouquet'. Just before the bride leaves to change for her honeymoon (inexplicably Jewish brides throw their bouquets *after* changing into going-away clothes) she mounts a staircase or dais and tosses her bouquet among the bridesmaids standing below; the girl who catches it will be the next bride. If no bouquet is carried the bride's floral fan or prayer-book markers are thrown instead. Bridegrooms sometimes toss their boutonnières among their ushers. In Europe the bride's bouquet has medicinal virtue, and it is said that three leaves from it will cure any fever.

The bride's floral wreath, worn upon her hair, signifies maidenhood; its destruction, the end of girlhood. Like the bouquet it may be thrown, this time among the guests, and to secure a fragment means early marriage. In Switzerland it is set alight by the *gelbe frau* or mistress of ceremonies at the wedding. Brisk burning is lucky; smouldering less so. The bride kneels in the 'ashes of maidenhood' and asks the company's blessing upon her marriage. In Kansas both veil and wreath were stitched in place upon the bride's hair and 'tying the bride' was an honour keenly sought by every woman in the community. Greek brides wore an evergreen wreath, expressing the quality they hoped their marriages were to show.

White roses symbolise virginity. In Normandy the bride wore in her hair a white rose and a small mirror framed in green silk: both were laid at the head of her bed on her wedding night, showing that maidenhood, the fading rose, was over. In Germany, until the nineteenth century, bridesmaids clubbed together to buy the bride's myrtle wreath; a Czech bride wore rosemary ceremonially woven for her on the wedding eve. It was often a matter of choosing a flower near to hand: in the Greek islands brides and maids chose wreaths of wild hyacinth.

Flowers express fertility and are seen at weddings in every part of the world. In Stuart England they were strewn in the bride's path as she walked to church:

> Full many maids, clad in their best array,
> In honour of the bride, come with their flaskets,
> Fill'd full of flowers, others in wicker baskets,
> Bring from the marsh rushes to o'erspread,
> The ground whereon to church the lovers tread.[25]

Today the 'flower girl', a small bridesmaid with a basket of petals, walks ahead of the bride and keeps the old tradition alive at American weddings, but actual strewing is now sometimes banned because the bridal party might slip on moist petals.

Until 1914 and the changes of World War I, popular brides in Shropshire were 'respected' with arches of evergreens, white paper gloves – sometimes a large and small glove hanging together – and pink paper hearts. The good-luck messages to be seen by the couple on their way to church expressed general good wishes; only when they were on their way home as man and wife was it safe to say 'Long Life and Happiness to A B. Esquire and His Lady'.[26]

Gloves were an emblem of maidenhood, and some see an agreeable sexual symbolism in them also. They were certainly freely exchanged by wedding guests, seizing their chances, presenting the favour (perhaps with a ribbon knot to wear at the wedding) with words such as 'Take away the "g" and make us a pair of loves.' A Pears soap advertisement of the nineteenth

century showed a pretty girl creeping upon tiptoe to kiss a
sleeping young man, with the caption 'Will she win the
gloves?'– her prize if the kiss could be bestowed so slyly that the
sleeper did not awake.

In America where weddings may take place in the bride's
home, flowers have special importance. White House weddings
have reflected changing floral tastes. When President Hayes'
niece, Emily Platt, married General Russell Hastings in 1878 in
the Blue Room, a marriage bell of 15,000 white buds and
blossoms, suspended by a rope of flowers, hung over their
heads: if petals from a floral bell fall upon a bride during the
marriage service she will never know a care. Eight years later
when President Cleveland married Frances Folsom, each
column of the East Room was decorated with the national arms
of the United States, with stripes of red and white roses, stars of
white roses and a field of blue immortelles. In the Blue Room,
where the ceremony took place, fireplaces were filled with
scarlet begonias (for flames), with grey-leafed centaureas (for
ashes) on hearths. One mantlepiece was decorated with light
and dark pansies, forming the date 2 June 1886; another bore the
monogram 'C/F' in red and white roses; a scroll of immortelles
in red, white and blue formed the legend *E Pluribus Unum*, the
motto of the United States. But by the wedding of Alice
Roosevelt in 1906, tastes had shifted; her flowers were mauve
azaleas, pale pink carnations, asparagus fern, American Beauty
and Bride roses, with a sunburst of Easter lilies, behind the
officiating Bishop Satterlee.

In many European countries it was customary until recent
years to plant a 'wedding tree', decorative or living, before the
house of the newly-weds, for luck. Round Lucerne,
Switzerland, the bridegroom set a pine tree decorated with
flowers and ribbons before his bride's door; she hung the
cherished tree from the window until her first child was born,
when its wood made the cradle. No Norman wedding was
complete without white-ribboned pine saplings forming a floral
arch on either side of the wedding house door. Pine is a tree
readily obtained, easy to cut, straight and trim, but its choice
was perhaps of more subtle origin, for both tree and cone had
phallic symbolism in the Roman cult of Venus and a pine-cone

under the pillow secures a husband's fidelity. In Holland the pot plant *Araucaria excelsa*, the Norfolk Island pine, is considered a traditional wedding present, but the custom must be of fairly recent origin as the plant was not introduced into Europe until the eighteenth century. It reinforces the old association of pine trees with weddings. At weddings in Burgundy a ribbon-decked laurel tree was hoisted to the highest chimney of the wedding house by the best man and six assistants. Then a bottle of brandy was broken over it and healths drunk as the guests sang:

> Il est planté, le laurier,
> Le bon vin l'arrose
> Qu'il amene aux mariés
> Ménage tout rose,
>   Tout rose!

In Czechoslovakia as late as 1937, a living tree, decorated with ribbons and coloured eggshells, was planted secretly by night at the bride's gate: it represented her life – she would live as long as her tree. Or the wedding tree may be strictly commemorative. Christopher Lawrence, the English silversmith, was commissioned recently to design a set of six goblets for a married couple, the design to include a magnolia leaf. On their wedding day, twenty years before, they had planted a magnolia in their garden; it was still flourishing and they wanted their happy marriage to be remembered by its leaf.[27]

'STEALING MISTRESS BRIDE': RELICS OF CAPTURE

Marriage by capture was the accepted way of winning a wife in the primitive world and many centuries later when the sport, long outlawed by the church, had degenerated into a good-humoured romp, traces of belligerence remained. In Iceland the very word for marriage is *brudlaup* or 'bride-run', and in Husaby church, Sweden, was preserved a set of torch-lances used when the bridegroom galloped off with his bride flung across his saddlebow after her capture by night.

Of a 'horse-wedding' in Wales in 1813 one observer wrote:

> The bride mounted behind her nearest kinsman, is carried off . . . pursued by the bridegroom and his friends with loud shouts. It is not uncommon . . . to see two or three hundred sturdy Cambro-Britons riding at full speed, crossing and jostling to the no small amusement of the spectators.[28]

and another recorded with feeling:

> Ill may it befall the traveller who has the misfortune of meeting a Welsh wedding on the road. He would be inclined to suppose that he had fallen in with a company of lunatics escaped from their confinement.[29]

Enjoyable opportunities for mock aggression and an escape for a few hours from the hard grind of peasant life were not lightly abandoned. In the late nineteenth century the Welsh horse-wedding was still in full swing in Cardiganshire. The bridegroom's party rode to the bride's house to be confronted by locked doors and spirited resistance from her friends. Scuffling and horseplay were followed by the *pwnco*, question and answer in verse, a witty contest between the parties perhaps lasting for several hours:

> *Bridegroom's party (outside):*
> We are coming on an errand
> From a warm-hearted young man
> To fetch your bright-eyed Annie
> To be his loving partner.
>
> *Bride's party (within the house):*
> If you intend proposing marriage
> You will get the answer from Annie
> That there is certainly great trouble
> In having a husband and a family.

But finally resistance was worn down, the bride's party conceding:

> It is better you should take her
> Than disappoint the lover's heart[30]

and admitting the bridegroom. But by then the bride had hidden, or had disguised herself in man's clothing, or as an old crone nursing a baby boy (to ensure sons for the marriage). Eventually she was carried off by the assault party, with her father, brothers and supporters in hot pursuit on horseback – every nag in the parish was pressed into service for bride-stealing. By careful design the bride's 'rescue' came just too late, and the party finally got to church.

A similar custom was found in Brittany, another Celtic country. There the frustrated bridegroom was held at bay for hours and the bagpipes played merrily while the bride was disguised first as the grandmother, then as the mistress of the house, then as a small child.[31] At Moslem weddings the bride's young relations still tease and harass the bridegroom and refuse him entry. Disguising the bride was an important time-gaining ruse. In the Tyrol a bride-doll was offered as first substitute; in Polonia a bearded man was produced as 'bride'; among the Saxons of Transylvania the disguised bride hid behind a curtain with two married friends and the bridegroom had to identify his bride with all three conspiring to confuse him. Half-serious 'hostility' is still to be seen in Languedoc, France, if the bridegroom is a 'foreigner'; in Spain and Switzerland the stranger had to 'buy his bride' by a gift of wine and meat to the young men of her village. These escapades were enthusiastically absorbed into American pioneer lore. Madam Knight wrote of an appealing variant of 'bride-stealing' in Connecticut in 1704:

> They generally marry very young; the males oftener as I am told under twenty years than above; they generally make public weddings and have a way something singular in some of them; viz. just before joining hands the Bridegroom quits the place, who is soon followed by the Bridesmen, and, as it were, dragged back to duty, being the reverse to the former practice among us to steal Mistress Bride.

'Bride-stealing' lingered into the eighteenth century in the Connecticut Valley, last outpost of many customs; slighted suitors, not invited to the wedding, held the kidnapped bride at a country tavern until the bridegroom redeemed her with a handsome supper for the thieves. The last bride stolen in Hadley, Massachusetts, was Mrs Job March in 1783.

Wedding customs still show the influence of capture. The gift (now often cufflinks or cigarette case) a bridegroom gives his best man recalls the reward given for his aid in the bride-fight; the gifts to the bridesmaids recall the bribes they received to persuade them to release the bride.

'There is perhaps no savage custom . . . which has so increased the gaiety of civilised nations as the common taboo between a man and his mother-in-law, one common to both primitive and sophisticated societies.'[32] Every comedian knows that the old joke still serves, and the Germans have enlarged it: 'schwiegermutter – teufelsunterfutter' and 'schwiegermutter – tigermutter'. The mother-in-law owes her unenviable reputation to marriage by capture, for inevitably she must be antipathetic to the new son-in-law who 'stole' her beloved child. Among the Roro of New Guinea the bride defends herself from would-be captors with hands, feet and teeth. In the midst of the uproar the bride's mother, armed with a garden tool or club, lashes at everyone within reach, howling curses upon the ravishers of her precious daughter.[33]

The honeymoon, too, recalls the past. After the deceits and manoeuvres of capture it was often politic for the young couple to hide for a 'moon' while parental tempers cooled. Far from being a pleasure trip, the honeymoon was a safety measure. Honeymooners today are as interested as they ever were in keeping their destination a secret.

THE WEDDING PROCESSION

Until the late nineteenth century, many bridal parties went to church on foot. Edwin Grey wrote of Hertfordshire, England, in the 1870s that if homes lay at the parish boundary couples might walk two or three miles to be married, with interested children as an escort and cottage women calling good wishes from their doors.[34] The party proceeded two by two –the old superstition that the pair must not meet on the wedding day before the ceremony had little weight where there was no alternative. It was lucky indeed if the best man and bridesmaids

A Tudor walking wedding at Hampton Lucy, Warwickshire

were married; less so if merely engaged: 'those who walk to church beforehand, will never walk as man and wife' was the old saying.

Group disguises helped to outwit evil wishers. Maids and men of the wedding party were dressed to resemble the couple. Today dresses of bride and maids still have common features: in Victorian prints and photographs, with all in white, it is difficult at a quick glance to tell who is who. Today, in the West at least, the best man, like the groom, may appear in uniform of morning dress with white carnation. At weddings of the 'Old Order Amish', members of the Mennonite community of the United States, which retains many of its sixteenth and seventeenth century ways, the couple and their attendants are dressed indistinguishably and only a close knowledge of the order of procession reveals their roles. To scare away evil spirits, two males keep the bridegroom between them wherever he may go on the wedding day; two girls protect the bride.[35] There is safety in numbers and uniformity but bridesmaids do not escape unscathed. 'Thrice a bridesmaid, never a bride' is a direct reference to the ill-wishing a bridesmaid so experienced will have absorbed.

'Sanding' the bride's path to church, about 1912, with decorative patterns and the motto 'Long life and happiness'. Sanding was a wedding custom unique to Knutsford, Cheshire. John Vernon, a noted sander, is shown as he completes his design (*Frank Vernon*)

When John Newcombe, a wealthy clothier of Newbury, Berkshire, married in 1597 in a ritual typical of Elizabethan England, a silver cup filled with wine (for richness to come) with a gilded, beribboned branch of rosemary (for remembrance and against sorcery) was carried before the bride. The bridesmaids held bridecakes and garlands of gilded wheat (for fertility) and the bride was led to church 'between two sweet boys, with Bride-laces and Rosemary tied about their silken sleeves'. (The presence of male children ensured sons for the marriage.)

In Bulgaria in the nineteenth century the bride and guests in horseback procession were led by a rider holding a flag surmounted by an apple. 'With the garlands of flowers, and vine leaves, their songs and strains of wild music, their gleeful shouts and gay laughter, this wedding procession presents the appearance of an ancient chorus of Bacchanals wending its way by mountain path and ravine to some old shrine of the vinous god.' As the party entered the village it was met by the best man, leading a goat with gilded horns, and carrying the bridal crowns, baskets of fruit, cakes and wine for the party, symbolising future wealth. According to the doctrine of sympathetic magic, to suggest wealth was to create it. After kissing her horse farewell on the forehead, the bride entered the wedding house where in the granary stood a wine barrel bearing the wedding cake and a glass of wine. The couple were married, tasted the wine, and walked three times round for luck, while fruit and comfits showered over them.

In Normandy the wedding procession, led by a fiddler, left for church in bright waggons or on horses gay with rosettes and scarlet harness (the finest witch-deterrent colour). The horses walked – to trot might seem irreverent before a sacrament, although *de rigeur* on the homeward journey – and the bride threw handfuls of coins to passers-by. To capture a coin was a happy augury.

Summing up the style of Yorkshire weddings in the mid-nineteenth century, Canon J. C. Atkinson wrote in *Forty Years in a Moorland Parish*:

The most typical Dales wedding I ever remember having witnessed was nearly forty years ago and on Martinmas Day. I should not have spoken of the event in the singular number, for there were in point of fact, four weddings, all to be solemnized co-incidentally. And, whether by arrangement or by chance, all four of the couples, with their attendants, came up to the church in one cavalcade. First, there were not less than seven horsemen, each with a pillion-borne female behind him. Three of these were brides; the others attendants. Of other attendants, male

Traditional bridal carriage, drawn by the traditional grey horses, at a wedding in Kent, 1974 Mr & Mrs Adrian Dawes; (*Jean Photographs*)

and female, there must have been at least as many more, and then came those who had gathered to see the wedding, and so forth. But besides, there were from a dozen and a score men, mostly young, who carried guns, and who, as the weddingers passed down the little slope leading to the churchyard gate, fired a salvo. As may be supposed, more than one or two of the horses, being neither sobered by age and hard work, nor yet trained to stand fire, were startled and began to plunge or rear. I fully expected a disaster. However, with the exception of one of the pillion ladies, who slid gently – though not without raising her voice – backwards down over the crupper of her steed, no casualty occurred.

Today a fortunate bride or groom sees a grey horse in road or field on the way to church. In the days of horse transport, grey horses were chosen for the bridal carriage if possible. (At Harpenden it was said that 'Ole Grey Will', an aged nag from the Railway Hotel, attended every wedding.) Among those keeping the tradition lively is Stroud Riding and Driving Stables in Gloucestershire, which provides carriages and matched grey horses for weddings. The horses wear orange blossoms and white satin rosettes, drivers and guards wear white carnations: posies are attached to lampholders. At first real flowers were used, but the horses had always tasted them before the wedding was over. The luckiest horseshoe to give a bride comes from the near hind foot of a grey mare but at weddings a silverfoil-covered cardboard horseshoe is substituted, attached to the bouquet, presented to the bride at the church door, or appearing on gift cards or as a cake decoration. The horseshoe's lunar shape makes it a growth and fertility symbol.

Beliefs attaching to horse-drawn bridal carriages were readily transferred to cars. The white-ribbon decorated bridal carriage must never be turned at the church gate, within sight of the couple, lest they suffer a 'reversal'. Chauffers of hired bridal cars still heed the old tradition. If the horses refused to start on the journey to church Jeremiahs wagged their heads; the match was doomed. Mechanical difficulties are just as ill-omened. A hired Rolls-Royce would not start at a recent Buckinghamshire wedding and the bride was late: 'Are we embarrassed?' said a mechanic at the garage, 'It's such bad luck for her.'

TEASING THE PARSON

Wedding parties were seldom subdued by ceremonial and snatched the chance to tease. At Gaillac, France, in Roman style, a rain of luck-giving nuts fell about the pair as they knelt at the altar. At Llanedy, in Wales, in the early nineteenth century, matters were out of hand. The parson, rather than the couple, was bombarded with an accurate salvo of nuts and apples. 'The easy-going clergyman would take no other notice of it than brushing these missiles off the open page of his prayer-book. But a young curate named Morris . . . put a sudden and final stop at such interruptions. At the first marriage that he celebrated, on being struck by some nuts, he looked up, marked a prominent offender, closed his book, jumped over the chancel rails, seized the man, and flung him neck and crop right through the window . . . .' The culprit suffered three broken ribs and not surprisingly the custom ceased forthwith. At Donington-on-Bain, Lincolnshire, all the old women of the parish, 'with an ardour unabated by the chill of age', tossed hassocks at the bridal party. All went well until about 1780 when the rector was accidentally hit by a flying hassock. Again the custom halted abruptly.

In Scotland and the north of England the parson, however shy, was expected to kiss the bride. A Durham lady, marrying away from home and banking upon the customary salute, 'after waiting for it in vain . . . boldly took the initiative and bestowed a kiss upon the astonished south country vicar'. Another clergyman was told by a dawdling bridal party 'Please sir, you've no kissed Mollie.' It was lucky to kiss the bride before her husband could do so, but if the parson were *not* shy there was another problem: a Scottish bridegroom stated the difficulty:

> It's no very decent for you to be kissing,
> It does not look well with the black coat ava,
> 'Twould hae set you far better tae hae gi'en us your blessing,
> Than thus by such tricks be breaking the law.
>
> Dear Wattie, quo' Robin, it's just an old custom,
> An' the thing that is common should ne'er be ill ta'en,
> For where ye are wrong, if you had na a-wished him,
> You should ha' been first. It's yoursel' is to blame!

5

THE WEDDING DAY: 2

MASTER FOR LIFE?

Marriage is a battlefield as much as an amicable partnership and charms determine who shall rule the roost. A Swedish bride secures supremacy by setting her right foot ahead of the bridegroom's at the altar rail and contriving to see him on the wedding day before he sees her. As a Syrian, Cypriot or Turkish couple arrive at their new home, one tries to tread upon the other's foot – the winner controls the household.

Leaving church was once less a moment for smiles and photography than for action. American brides believed that whichever of the pair made the first purchase after marriage would rule – and swiftly bought a pin from a bridesmaid at the churchdoor. At a wedding in Orange City, New Jersey, about 1890, a spectator remarked that it was a pity that the bride had stepped over the church doorsill with her left foot for 'Now she'll always be under his thumb.' In Scotland, at double weddings, the first couple to get out of church would walk off with the blessing and unseemly scuffles were common. In the Vosges the leading couple's reward would be a boy as their first child.

Some gestures towards mastery were more disciplinary than magical: a Russian bride presented her husband with a whip she had made herself and he struck her lightly three times, saying: 'I love thee like my soul, but beat thee like my fur cloak.'

Among the Mussulmans of Sindh a contest decides the knotty question of household leadership. If the bridegroom can, with one hand only, seize a date grasped firmly in the bride's fist, he will rule; otherwise he is doomed to henpecking. If the Scandinavian bride can trap her new husband into picking up her dropped handkerchief her triumph is complete and he will 'bend his back all his life'. A sheep is often included among the bridegroom's betrothal gifts in Morocco; the bride adorns herself in ritual makeup, climbs upon the surrogate's back and urges it forward, saying:

> If I tell thee to move, go on,
> If I say hold, then stop,
> If I tell thee to sleep, then slumber,
> If I bid thee wake, open thine eyes.

She next plucks a little wool from the sheep's head, mouth, belly and tail and binds it into a magical sachet which is secretly hidden away. Its preservation, she believes, maintains her ascendancy. But the charm, although powerful, can be overturned. When the Moroccan husband first enters his wife's bedroom, he carries his right slipper in his hand; she, armed with her own slipper, awaits him. They both strike out: whoever gets in the first blow will dominate the household. In China the bridegroom has the advantage if he can sit upon a part of his wife's dress as they seat themselves upon the bridal bed. She, of course, does her best to anticipate him.

Obviously these charms can have no intrinsic effect on the household's true hierarchy: but like much magic they are an important part of a psychological battle of wits. The successful practitioner is made confident, the loser demoralised – surely an important step along the road to marital mastery?

FERTILITY

Until fifty years ago (and the subject, although little discussed today, is probably far from defunct in many communities) fertility charms were all-important to the married and about-to-be married. Childbearing was the principal reason for matrimony: by the doctrine of imitative magic the bride was brought into contact with babies, seeds and objects connected with animal reproduction, or with ancient stones linked with supplications. This, it was felt, could do nothing but good. Her own reproductive powers would be stimulated.

At Roman weddings nuts were thrown for fertility and many centuries later were still strewn at wedding breakfasts in France.

Basket of nuts for a Devon bride

Devon brides received baskets of hazelnuts as they left church; in Germany 'going a-nutting' was a euphemism for lovemaking and in the English tradition the devil would bend down the branches for girls who nutted on Sundays and would see that they went to the altar pregnant: 'The baby would come before the ring.' A good crop of nuts traditionally precedes one of babies ('plenty of nuts, plenty of cradles') and double nuts portend twins. The name 'nuts' for testicles has age-old symbolism and in a case of attempted murder in Wiltshire, England, in 1974, the accused husband was alleged to have called his wife's lover 'the village nutter'.[36]

There are many connections between nuts and fertility: almond paste ('called 'matrimony' since it blends sweet and bitter flavours) commonly appears on wedding cakes. In Italy pink and white sugared almonds, important as bridecake elsewhere, are generously distributed in ornamental boxes; in 1956 British guests unable to attend an Italian wedding were sent white sugared almonds wrapped in white veiling within a little tray. An almond tree will always fruit well near the home of a bride: and the tree at White Lodge, Windsor, bore a heavy crop in 1893 when Princess May of Teck was leaving for

Buckingham Palace, as a bride. In Thuringia a shelled almond is dropped into the wedding soup and whoever retrieves it will marry next. And at gipsy weddings in Albacete, Spain, everyone heaps pink almond blossoms over the bride's head as she dances. The Chinese wife is offered chestnuts and ju-jubes: conveniently these words form the wish 'Have a son soon'.

Seeds are obvious carriers of new life and suitable offerings for brides. Bulgarian matrons present the new wife with dried figs, their multitudinous seeds promising many children. The connection of figs with fertility is ancient; in Greek mythology Priapus was god of reproduction and his statues, set up in gardens to encourage crops, were always of fig wood. In Greece, Syria and Rhodesia the pomegranate – another many-seeded fruit – plays the role of baby-simulator and the bride scatters the seeds as if by distributing them she brings countless progeny nearer. In Somerset an onion, famous in folk-medicine for promoting both health and increase, was thrown after the bride with the wish that she would enjoy a large family. Probably the many seeds of the onion seemed helpful: North American Indian men believe that such seed increases the production of sperm.

Cereal grains (and their modern substitute, confetti) are customarily thrown at weddings – even if their users do not realise that they are indulging in a fertility ritual. Medical science has given a new slant to the old association, for some authorities now believe that vitamin E, found in wheatgerm and cereals, is connected with human fertility. In Nottinghamshire until about 1890, wheat signified prosperity also; guests called 'Bread for life and pudding for ever!' as golden wheat showered over the newlyweds, and until recent years in Burgundy in the 'sowing of the married pair' wheat was tossed from the upper windows, to:

> Scarcity and want shall shun you,
> Ceres' blessing now is on you.

Fish produce abundant eggs and young and have a high reputation among traditional love foods. Oriental Jewish brides step three times over a basin containing two live fish, while witnesses repeat 'Be fruitful and multiply'.[37] In America today, dishes such as smoked white fish, sable carp, smoked salmon and gefillte fish figure largely on the menus of Jewish weddings, in maintenance of the old belief.

Like produces like: the wise bride had babies about her as she married. A Swedish bride even had an infant boy to sleep in her bed on the night before the wedding, to induce the swift conception of a son and brides newly arrived home in Turkey, Russia and Yugoslavia were handed a baby to caress with the wish 'May you be a happy mother'. Conversely if a woman were anxious *not* to conceive she must take care that none of her friends lays a baby down upon her bed; if they did the results would be disastrous. A gipsy woman desiring children drinks water into which her husband has spat, for saliva, like semen, is a vital secretion and the words 'the spitting image of his father' are full of reproductive significance.

Hen and egg are other obvious agents of fertility. The modern preference for free-range, farm eggs, fertilised by the cock and claimed therefore to be of extra potency and food value, is an oblique offshoot of the old superstition. In Scotland a cackling hen was tossed into the house before the newlyweds entered; in Borneo the bridegroom is sprinkled with the blood of a cock, the bride with that of a hen. Moroccan Jews throw eggs at the bride so that she may bear as easily and prolifically as a fowl. The Mussulmans of Sindh seat the bride upon an overturned basket imprisoning a brood of chickens. She rises, the chickens escape and the number she can catch with her hands shows the number of children she will have. A Transylvanian gipsy husband with a barren wife blows the contents of an egg into her mouth. The belief that conception may be achieved by mouth is ancient and one still hears of simple girls who fancy themselves pregnant after a kiss.

Stone circles and standing stones or menhirs (often for phallic worship) were aids to fertility. At Carnac, France, a childless couple visited the menhir at full moon; they stripped and, naked, the husband chased the wife round the stones until he caught her and they had sexual intercourse in the rock's shadow. In Europe running and leaping naked through the fields was a common crop stimulant and there are stories too of such charms in the rural United States at planting time. Similar rites at Kerréatous, Brittany, left a woman confident of managing her husband successfully and a man of begetting sons. Certain flat rocks and megaliths in Ireland are 'beds of Diarmid and Gráinne', where the legendary lovers slept while eluding the Finn and the Fiana: travellers have reported the embarrassment of local girls asked to guide visitors to the stones, for by tradition if a girl accompanies a strange man to such a spot she may deny him no favour. Barren women and their husbands sleep upon the 'beds' to encourage conception.

In simulated birth barren wives forced their bodies through the holed Kelpie Stone or Needle in the swift-flowing and turbulent River Dee, near Dinnet, Scotland, in the hope of becoming 'joyful mothers'. This was no light ordeal: the hole was about 18 inches in diameter. One unfortunate woman accomplished the feat but there was no result. It was then remembered by her advisers that she must make the passage in the same direction as the current. This she did and conception followed. Couples who sit upon the stone 'St Fiacre's chair' at Monceaux, France, are assured of children.[38] Another rock near Athens is worn smooth as polished ivory by the numberless brides who have sat naked upon it, hoping for sons. In all these charms, skin-to-stone contact is essential.

The unequivocally male and perhaps Romano-British figure of the Cerne Giant, carved with explicitly delineated sexual organs upon the hillside turf of the village of Cerne Abbas, Dorset, makes husbands who sit upon him strong. Girls and wives fearful of losing husbands and lovers take their problems to the giant and walk round his outline as a prophylactic charm. Before marriage many women visit the giant as a matter of course to assure the future; some recommend that the couple spend the night on the relevant portion of the figure's anatomy for fully effective magic, and belief in the giant's efficacy is still lively in surrounding villages.

Although today large families are no longer commendable, barrenness may remain a disgrace. A childless Moroccan woman, for example, is scorned all her life as a sterile 'mule'. Mules are dangerous beasts: in the Ozarks a girl who rides one will never get her man. The barren have always taken remedial

Aerial view of the Cerne giant, Dorset, England (*The National Trust*)

steps and Cambridgeshire couples slept with the testicle of a castrated stallion under their pillows as a charm. If a Moroccan man is blamed for the unfruitfulness, he eats the testicles of a sheep, if a woman, she eats those of a cock. In the Languedoc, France, the skin of a recently-lambed ewe is laid over the would-be mother's head. Such procedures transfer the virility and fecundity of animals and birds to the supplicants.

In hard times charms inhibit breeding. Fertile nuts promote births and by the doctrine of opposites, 'dead' or roasted nuts prevent them: Rumanian brides not wanting children hid in their bodices as many roasted nuts as they wished years of childlessness. North African women eat barley fallen from the mouth of a mule, or munch a fig so dry that it will not germinate; negroes of the American South rely upon an explosive mixture of gunpowder in milk to impede conception. In Cambridgeshire, mothers of large families held the hand of a dead man – a thing of death, not life – or laid under their pillows 'corpse money' which had rested in his mouth. This would prevent further births, but if a husband found these coins and announced in the village inn that he was funding his drinking thus, he was given free beer!

APHRODISIACS AND FIDELITY CHARMS

Today the aphrodisiac trade is enjoying an unprecedented boom. In Europe 'strengthening mixtures' are seen as part of every drug-store display: in the southern United States in particular, sales are brisk among both white and negro populations of 'love powders' (male – pink, female – white), brimstone, lodestone, sassafras, asafoetida, resin – traditional components of charms for seducing girls, tethering husbands and bringing dilatory lovers up to scratch. Some rebarbative charms, made of grave dirt, feathers, hair, blood or powdered human bones, dried frogs and snakeskin – the *materia medica* of voodoo – are carried on the person, wrapped in red flannel within little scented leather bags, and their power is never underestimated. In the Ozark mountains such 'ju-jus' or 'conjures' are regarded so seriously that their victims are held blameless: were they not controlled by others more powerful than they? Deserted wives are consoled by the thought that wandering husbands were 'conjured off' and did not depart of their own free will.

The fidelity charm too is still in considerable use. An American negro charm of the south requires a hair from the woman's head and a little of her pubic hair. The man slips from bed and pokes the hair into a crack in wall or floor nearby and the charm ensures that his wife will never leave him. In north Devon, 'still liquors' brewed from wheat and herbs revived tired men after a hard day on the farm, and 'kept them near their wives'; 'matched cider'– prepared by burning a brimstone taper within the half-full barrel – was said by the old folks to 'make girls feel cuddly';[39] brimstone is an ancient love-charm ingredient. Wives in Carolina hold straying husbands by driving a hickory 'stob' into the doorpost: hickory is a wood slow to rot, and while the peg is sound, husbands remain faithful. Other women sew a little of their own and their husbands' pubic hair into a sachet to be worn in the clothing as a fidelity charm. Coat collars are favourite repositories.

The doctrine of signatures, developed in the fifteenth century, 'signed' or attached many plants by colour, shape or habit to a specific condition or disease. From this doctrine the oriental ginseng, *Panax schinseng*, from Chinese for 'man-shape', a highly regarded aphrodisiac, derives its reputation. It is said to boost the waning sexual powers of ageing men; but its users are likely to be disappointed, for most medical authorities report that ginseng is at best an appetite stimulant, with no effect on other functions. Any benefit felt must be psychological. But despite such pronouncements ginseng's reputation is undimmed: sales constantly increase. In Germany 50,000 bottles of ginseng mixtures are sold annually by one company alone. The prime section of the oriental root –'heaven-grade'– sells at up to $40 per ounce: average roots weigh an ounce each and are about three inches long, often forked, naturally or by judicious trimming, into a rough human form, with arms, legs and, with luck, penis. By the doctrine of signatures ginseng must therefore benefit man.

For thousands of years this plant, taken medicinally and carried on the person, has been the 'root of life' to the Chinese. An unbroken root of shaped ginseng, encased in silk, set in a jewelled casket and costing from $300–$400, is an appropriate gift for an old man. It is a common belief that a man who has lost his sexual powers – his 'manhood'– will die within the year, although one man of 93 who admitted believing this in his younger years said that experience had proved it wrong! American ginseng (*Panax quinquefolius*) is also valuable, and although it is now rare there are stories of secret patches profitably cultivated in the Ozark mountains.

The mandrake is another plant of ancient reputation

A mandrake root in human form

('provocative to venery' said Sir Thomas Browne). There is much confusion between the true mandrake, *Atropa mandragora*, the American mandrake, mayapple or raccoonberry, and the English mandrake, the white briony. Other plants are also substituted and probably very little of the 'mandrake' sold in herbal shops today is *A. mandragora*. The Greeks called the plant *anthropomorphum*, the Romans *semi-homo*, for its human form; the Arabs, 'devil's testicles' after its paired fruits. The belief in mandrake's effect on conception is as ancient as the story of Reuben, Rachel and Leah in Genesis. In the period of Henry VIII briony roots were trained in moulds into little man-shaped figures, with sprouted millet for hair and beards. Italian ladies paid as much as 30 gold ducats for such 'puppettes' or 'mammettes' which brought sexual energy, conception and luck in love. Mandrake is still considered a fertility stimulant and its roots are tied to bedposts or scraped into water and taken medicinally. In the markets of the Middle East amulets of mandrake are sold as aids to virility; in Cambridgeshire, England, mandrake was often hung in cottage bedrooms to induce large families, and today orthodox Jews of New York and Chicago still import large quantities of mandrake roots which, according to shape, are deemed male or female and taken accordingly.

The tomato too has a sexual reputation. When the plant was brought from South America to North Africa and finally to France it was called *la pomme du Moor* – interpreted by Englishmen as *la pomme d'amour*, so that its career as an ingredient of love potions began forthwith. ('Tomatoes are cheaper, now's the time to fall in love,' sang Eddie Cantor in the 1930s.) The juice of the 'love apple' was – and perhaps still is – slipped into the drinks of torpid lovers, and today nutritionists identify an element in the tomato which increases fertility and virility, and believe there may be a grain of truth in the old superstition.

Lettuce, wild and cultivated, was also thought to have the power of arousing love and of promoting childbearing if eaten by a wife. It was a customary ingredient of medieval love-philtres. As sometimes occurs, the belief became inverted: by the seventeenth century it was said that lettuce 'represses venereous dreams' if applied to the testicles. It was prescribed for those suffering from satyriasis and nymphomania, or those not desiring children. By the nineteenth century the belief was stated quite emphatically: 'O'er much lettuce in the garden will prevent a young wife's bearing.' Then the superstition seemed to revert to its original form, and in 1951 a correspondent wrote to the *Daily Mirror*, of London, that after several childless years she and her husband had been advised by their doctor to eat plenty of lettuce. Within six months she had conceived. Lettuce juice is a very mild substitute for opium, producing a languorous drowsiness and a sense of relaxation and wellbeing. On this perhaps rests its reputation as a promoter of love, and indirectly of fertility.

In the English Fenland, tansy tea made from *Tanacetum vulgare* was the fertility drink, for the plant grows freely near rabbit burrows and rabbits are paragons of productivity. Similarly, in the Ozarks the fat found round the kidneys of wild rabbits in fall is a specific for sexual debility, and the patient who eats it will acquire the sexual energy of the rabbit. It is an old country joke that parsley grows best 'where petticoats rule'. Men

wanting sons were depressed by an over-lush patch of parsley in
their gardens, for it meant that female influences reigned to the
point where no boys would be born to the family. No man of
resolution permitted much parsley to flourish unhindered for
long!

ILLWISHING AND IMPOTENCE

Sterility and impotence are often ascribed to magic and ill-
wishing. 'Get knotted' is no innocent taunt, for the surest means
of rendering a man impotent is to leave a knot about his
garments with the muttered 'binding curse'–'may you have no
sons!'. In the Pitt Rivers Museum, Oxford, is a black and white
tape with twenty-three knots, each pierced with a black and
white pin. The charm was found in a mattress at 43 Strada
Meszoal, Valletta, Malta, earlier this century: it had been
pushed to the centre from a hole in the foot of the mattress, and
was thought to be the work of a disgruntled servant bent on
condemning his master to impotence.

As a Syrian bridegroom dresses for his wedding, helpers
search carefully among his clothes to confirm that no knot is
tied nor button fastened about him. An enchanter has but to slip
a knotted handkerchief into the bridegroom's pocket to produce
impotence. Moroccan men are terrified of this charm of erotic
witchcraft – the *aiguillette*, knot or *tqaf* –'locking up'–and carry
gum arabic against it. The mere suggestion that the spell has
been worked causes impotence through emotional tension, and
a sorceress is always on hand on the wedding night to 'untie'
any impeding knot. Wedding guests are closely watched lest
one should maliciously tie knots in a string during the
ceremony. Knot charms can be of considerable sophistication: a
wife may desire her husband's impotence only with her harem
rivals, not with herself, and a partial affliction only is arranged.
In Scotland in the eighteenth century every knot about the
clothing of bride or groom – garters, shoes and petticoats – was
carefully loosened before the ceremony and afterwards the
couple retired round separate corners to adjust their dress before
processing home. Today the Persian bride still sits facing Mecca
with all her clothes unfastened. Locking a padlock during the

marriage service was another trick to make consummation of the marriage impossible: the bride's hymen would thus be made impenetrable.

BARRING THE WAY: RITES OF PASSAGE

The moment of leaving church, the couple's first public appearance as man and wife, is marked by rites of passage, emphasising their new lives. In Britanny, until this century, neighbourhood beggars plaited hedgerow briars across the couple's path from church and only removed them when bribed. Village children in Japan hold the couple to ransom with straw ropes. In Somerset a flower rope greeted the popular, tin cans the rest. Ambitious obstructionists in old New England and the pioneer north-west of America even felled trees or stretched stout vines before the bridal carriage. Barring the way flourishes yet in Cardiganshire and Carmarthenshire, and when the Hon Bridget Assheton and William Worsley married at Downham Church, Lancashire, in 1956, the couple and their 500 guests were held captive by children at the church gate and only released after gifts of money had been made.

Guards of honour may greet newlyweds at the church door. Here there is double purpose: an act of respect from fellow-officers or friends, and a symbolic archway through which the pair enter married life. Swords form the arch if the bridegroom is a member of the armed forces, oars or golfclubs for a sportsman, or appropriate tools of his trade – T squares for draughtsmen, hoes for gardeners, truncheons for policemen. It is significant, in keeping with a true passage rite, that only the couple, never the wedding party, passes through the archway.

Sometimes an obstacle stood ready for the couple to leap. Leaping at weddings could well be related to the planting rituals of Europe, as well as being a passage rite. Typically, on 5 June 1873, at Bamburgh, Northumberland, the whole wedding party hopped over a carpet-covered stool at the church gate. By negotiating this 'petting stool' the bride showed acceptance of her new life and left 'pets' or tempers behind her: a stumble boded ill for domestic peace. Brides on Holy Island still negotiate the 'petting stone' in the churchyard. Such passage rites may precede or follow the ceremony: on the island of Karpathos in the Dodecanese, newlyweds break a rod laid across their door.

An indispensable part of the Orthodox Jewish marriage ceremony is the shattering by the bridegroom's heel of a wineglass, to shouts of 'Mazletouv!'–'Good luck!' from the guests. This ceremony may symbolise the breaking of the couple's former ties, or the bride's hymen, or typify the scattering of the Jewish people. All these explanations are offered, but it is probably just another passage rite.

BELLS, FEATHERS AND GUNPOWDER

At life's transitional moments, birth, marriage and death, individuals are most vulnerable to attack from ever-watchful demons. The movement from one life state to another weakens the normally protective personal aura. From earliest times powerful protective magic has been in use at weddings. Noise (the louder the better) intimidates the spirit world. Historically this din has been provided by bells and guns, but since these are unavailable or unacceptable in North American cities today, the latest in a long succession of protective sounds, a concerto of car horns, is heard as bridal parties leave church in ribbon-decorated cars. In 1974 the Metropolitan Toronto Parks Department considered complaints about the six or eight wedding parties which, with retinues of photographers, converged noisily together upon James Gardens on Saturday afternoons in the wedding season, despite 'No Excessive Horn Blowing' signs, the racket was clearly heard half a mile away. 'You'll have to put the sign in four languages,' Controller Gus Harris said, for the custom is particularly popular with immigrants from Europe.

In Britain, wedding peals are rung on churchbells everywhere. If a member of the ringing team marries, the peal is a 'wedding compliment'. At Aldington, Worcestershire, even in the 1920s the belfry was decorated with mutton and beef bones from feasts provided for the bellringers by grateful bridegrooms.[40] On one long-remembered day at Peterchurch, Herefordshire, ringers denied their expected reward revenged themselves by 'ringing the bells backwards'; proper ringing brought safety and luck but backwards ringing was a forceful ill-wish. Bells spoke portentously of the match: in another Worcestershire village about 1857 the great bell was set gently moving on the evening of the wedding day to 'fore-tell' the number of children the newly-married couple might expect. 'On this particular occasion,' wrote a visitor, 'the clapper was made to smite the bell thrice three times. The bride and bridegroom know, therefore, what to expect, and can make the needful preparations for the advent of their tuneful nine.'

Fireworks, gongs, ships' sirens, foghorns, have joined the orchestra. The Brahmin wedding procession comes home at night waving lamps to frighten the malevolent away. In the United States gunshots accompanied weddings until the nineteenth century. The Scottish-Irish Presbyterians of Londonderry, New Hampshire, fired salutes at daybreak on the wedding morning, again as the bridegroom rode to the bride's house: on every side his party was greeted with cheerful volleys. In Yorkshire in 1890 the old ladies of the village found 'some ancient flint-lock, horse-pistol or blunder-buss, which they discharged, with the muzzle resting on the windowsill. Near the house in which the bridal feast is spread, stand three or four men, with guns crammed to the muzzle with feathers, and as the party passes them, the guns are discharged and the air filled with falling feathers, thereby betokening a wish that nothing harder may ever fall on the happy pair.'[41]

In an explosive innovation at St Harmons, Radnorshire, in 1878, fog-signals placed on the railway line were satisfyingly detonated by the noon train just as the bridal party emerged from church and as late as 1910 it was the custom at Aylsham, Norfolk, for the blacksmith to explode gunpowder on his anvil, giving the bride a 'good wish' as the wedding party passed his forge.

RACES FOR GARTER, BROSE AND BOTTLE

Wedding races from church to bridehouse, on foot or horseback – or in Kansas by horse and buggy – were an important wedding event until fifty years ago, and another

A bride's garter from Yorkshire, dated 1749. Decorations are the couple's zodiacal signs of Venus, Jupiter, Virgo and Leo; initials were added in the blank spaces

reminder of the days of bride-capture. Prizes were the bride's garter, a ribbon (called a 'garter' if it decorously replaced it), a bottle of liquor, a bridecake – or the key to the bridal chamber itself! The value of the prize was unrelated to the pleasures of the race.

In colonial New Hampshire, as in Ireland, the race was 'running for the bottle'. A champion from each group rode a daredevil race over bad roads to the bride's house, where the winner seized the beribboned bottle of rum and turned to meet the advancing bridal party. The bottle was quickly passed round and the bridegroom flung the last drops to the ground as a libation, appeasing unknown gods.

Brose was a Scottish prize: Atholbrose – whisky and honey – or a homely oatmeal soup. It was remembered that the Rev William Porteous, of Kilbucho, Peebleshire, always exclaimed at the end of his wedding services, almost as part of them, 'Noo lads, tak' the gait, an' let's see what amang you will win the brose!' A savoury cabbage *kail* was another North Country prize – its winner would be first to marry. *The Collier's Wedding*, a Northumberland dialect poem of 1764, told how

> Four rustic fellows wait the while,
> To kiss the bride at the church-style:
> Then vig'rous mount their felter'd steeds,
> With heavy heels and clumsy heads,
> To scourge them going, head and tail –
> To win what country calls the *Kail.*

'Running for the broth' is still a popular wedding sport in County Down, Ireland. In Bavaria, until World War I, the winner of the race received the wooden 'key' of the bridal chamber. In Yorkshire he was actually shown into the room, where he turned back the bedclothes to bring luck to the newlyweds, before returning at a gallop to greet the bride with a tankard of warm ale. As late as 1890 the race for the bridecake was run in Anglesey, starting at the very moment the bride received her ring. Enthusiasm was so great that earlier in the century thirty young men had raced four miles for the prize.

A garter race in Yorkshire in 1820 is recorded thus:

> Lady –, a great stickler after old customs, on stepping from her bridal coach, enquired who had won the race. 'Ah did, my lady,' answered one of the stable-lads. Ascending the steps, her ladyship stepped half-over the threshold, calling out to the lad, 'come Tom and claim your prize!' adding, as she raised her silken gown, 'I intend to be properly married, and to have the luck I am entitled to.' Then, turning to the young fellow, smiling, she added 'Take it off, Tom, and give it to your sweetheart, and may it bring luck to both of you.'[42]

Such racing could endanger life and limb: safety was the last thought in the minds of weddingers, and strangers accidentally caught up in the throng were rightly alarmed. One noted with feeling:

> Nothing can be compared to it in wildness and obstreperous mirth. The bride and bridegroom may possibly be a little subdued, but their friends are like men bereft of reason. They career round the bridal party like Arabs of the desert, galloping over ground on which, in cooler moments, they would hesitate even to walk a horse – shouting all the time, and firing volleys from the guns they carry with them . . .[43]

Garter races survived until within living memory. *The Times*, 9 April 1910, reported an open-air wedding on the grassy slopes of the hills between England and Scotland. The bride lived in the English county of Cumberland about fifty yards from the border stream; the bridegroom was a Roxburgh shepherd. Although English law prohibits marriage ceremonies in private houses the bride particularly wished to be married at her home, and a compromise was reached: a Scottish minister performed the ceremony in the open air, on Scottish soil, just over the stream, and after 'the customary young men's race' had been run, the party crossed back into Cumberland for the wedding breakfast.

THE WEDDING CAKE

Eating and drinking together, vital to all weddings, marks the incorporation of the newlyweds into fresh social groups. Negotiation, argument, purchase now lie behind: co-operation and sharing are the order of the day. The ritual sampling and exchanging of good things spreads fortune and fertility from guests to couple, from couple to guests, and all profit from the prime sentiment of the feast.

In America the couple feed each other with the first slice of wedding cake: at Moslem weddings they each bite into the same sweetmeat. Sharing once had deeper meaning and in Elizabethan Jersey, in the Channel Islands, the marriage contract only became legally binding if the parties ate or drank together and pledged one another. After this its breaking was a matter for lawyers. In France the couple drink from the two-handled gold or silver *coupe de mariage*, engraved with dates and initials and preserved for later generations. The whole Japanese wedding ceremony turns upon sharing: within the shrine the couple drink the *san-san-ku-do* or 'three times three', taking nine sips from tiered cups and becoming man and wife at the first sip. And at the wedding feast the married pair drink hot perfumed *sake* from a little Satsuma kettle, decorated with small paper butterflies, to ensure that they are blessed with children. The kettle's double spout signifies that they intend to share everything in life. During the marriage ceremony of the Eastern Orthodox Church the bride and groom drink three times from a cup of wine, symbolising their willingness to sample the same cup of experience.

Sharing is just as important for wedding guests and the good influences of the feast are spread by giving them food to take home. At the royal wedding in 1959 of the Crown Prince of Japan and Princess Michiko, at each place stood a beautifully arranged wooden gift box, tied with red and white silk cords and holding boiled *tai* (sea bream), decorated with a gold quill, fish sausage, wild duck, salmon galantine, sweet chestnuts and bean paste.[44] And at the wedding in 1923 of Prince Albert (later George VI) and Lady Elizabeth Bowes-Lyon, guests were given pâtisserie in sugar baskets to take away.

The wedding cake is one of the oldest nuptial rites, in evidence from Roman times. When in its modern form it spread from France in the seventeenth century there were two cakes, a rich, substantial 'fruit-full' groom's cake, and a lighter bride's cake, gay with spun sugar ornaments. Today these cakes may be combined, or the groom's cake completely forgotten. In America, for example, a white, chocolate or lemon wedding-cake mixture, tiered, white-iced and decorated, is now popular. One psychologist has pronounced this change a manifestation of a matriarchal society, but appearances also enter into it for a rich fruit cake is far less imposing than the same weight of white cake. Sometimes the groom's cake survives in part: lower layers of white cake – the so-called 'lady's cake'– are eaten at the reception and the upper fruit tiers stored away for later occasions.

The separate groom's cake was commonly seen in America until about thirty years ago and, precut by the caterer, was packed in white satin, initialled heart-shaped boxes and carried home by guests as 'dreaming bread'. Fragments beneath pillows assured dreams of future mates. At present prices, however, this second cake is a luxury, although some brides, mindful of the old custom, give their guests silver-monogrammed paper napkins in which to carry away a little of the bride's cake in the old style.

In England a greater part of the tradition has survived. Wedding cakes are still nearly always of fruit mixture, representing the groom's cake, their white icing and decorations representing the bride's cake. Boxed cake goes to those unable to attend the wedding, so that they too may share in the luck, and part of the cake is preserved for anniversaries or christenings. Many wedding parties over the years must have enjoyed Mrs Beeton's 'Rich Bridecake' (in fact the groom's portion of the cake), calling for:

5 lbs. of the finest flour, 3 lbs. of fresh butter, 5 lbs. of currants, 2 lbs. of sifted loaf sugar, 2 nutmegs, $\frac{1}{4}$ oz. of mace, $\frac{1}{4}$ oz. of cloves, 16 eggs, 1 lb. of sweet almonds, $\frac{1}{2}$ lb. of candied citron, $\frac{1}{2}$ lb. each of candied orange and lemon peel, 1 gill of wine, 1 gill of brandy.[45]

Bermuda retains the full distinction of cakes: a three-tiered bridecake, with snow-white icing brushed with silver leaf (for the bride's purity and fertility) topped by a tree seedling, and the groom's single-layer rich dark cake, decorated with gold leaf (for the gold and goods with which he endows his bride). Ivy wreaths circling the cakes emphasise the couple's affection.

The four-foot high bridecake at the wedding of the Marquess of Kildare and Lady Caroline Leveson Gower in Staffordshire, England, 1847. Decorations are Irish harps and shamrocks (the marquess was an Irish peer) and a basket of white roses held by cupids

(To the ancient Greeks ivy symbolised the indissoluble bond of marriage.) The seedling is planted at the wedding reception, usually held at dusk on sweeping lawns, often with lights strung among the trees, perhaps those planted by the bride's parents and grandparents on their wedding days. Bermuda cedars were once a favourite wedding tree: today casuarinas or poincianas are often substituted.

Traditional wedding-cake decorations of doves, bells, cupids, orange blossoms, white roses and horseshoes have been joined in recent years by decorations expressing the couple's interests. Cakes have been adorned with tennis rackets, motor racing flags, violins, or toy soldiers, although the traditional bride and groom dolls remain firm favourites also. When Governor Ronald Reagan married in California, his wedding cake duplicated in sugar his life-sized portrait and Jack Webb, the actor, chose a cake entirely covered with police badges in coloured icing. Queen Victoria's wedding cake bore the traditional cupids and a figure of Britannia. Ring cakes – in the shape of the wedding ring, iced as such and with the couple's initials in silver, are popular in America. Lucky trinkets – a heart, coin, wishbone, thimble, button, ring or other favours – are still sometimes hidden in wedding cakes and their finders are assured of the traditional rewards of money, marriage and luck. At Prince Albert's wedding the bride pulled forward by broad satin ribbons a precut slice of the nine-foot wedding cake which contained seven (a lucky number in its own right) pure gold charms: and observers reported with some amusement that sedate and elderly courtiers jostled with the rest in the hope of getting a slice with a trinket.[46]

A bride should never bake her own wedding cake; this brings bad luck. But with the groom's help she cuts the first slice of cake herself, or she will be childless and every guest must join her in eating a little after she and the groom have exchanged and eaten a few crumbs. To taste the cake beforehand forfeits a husband's love, but a fragment preserved ensures his lifelong fidelity. A bridesmaid who carries wedding cake in her pocket until the honeymoon is over will soon marry. After the first wedding in a family, part of the cake must be kept in the house until all the unmarried daughters are wed, or they are doomed

Cutting a Canadian wedding cake with the historic Rogers sword (*Mrs Douglas Jennings*)

to spinsterhood. The sword or knife used to cut the cake is decorated with tulle bows, wax orange blossoms and a festoon of white satin ribbons. American brides often preserve the silver cake knife, suitably engraved with date and initials, as an heirloom for their daughters. One Canadian family cuts all its wedding cakes with the historic Rogers sword, brought to Canada from England in 1780 by Major Robert Rogers of the Rogers' Rangers. In the past few years, while in the keeping of Mrs Douglas Jennings of Toronto, the sword has cut no fewer than twelve wedding cakes, and although no records have been kept, probably hundreds over the past century.

WEDDING FEAST AND DANCE

The wedding feast is rich in its own traditions. In Normandy the bride kissed all the men as they entered and the groom kissed the girls. At a village wedding about 1930 at Ste Ursule, the feast was set in a great earth-floored barn. Each guest provided his own knife and fork. A woman from a neighbouring village, famous for her wedding luncheons, prepared rabbits, ducks, chickens, turkey, fish and mutton, and serving the eight or nine courses (with each dish passing righthanded to honour the sun) took many hours. The bridegroom assisted, distinguished by a white ribbon swinging from his left shoulder, laying the first cut of all the meats before his wife as tradition demanded. (If the bride wishes to be happy she must taste and share with her husband a little of every dish served at the wedding feast.) For twenty-four hours there was little concern for anything but eating and drinking, though there were customary interludes. The elderly assistant cooks entered to intone the solemn 'bride's song', soberly recalling life's fleeting years; then at a secret signal a small boy crept gleefully beneath the table to snatch the bride's garter, fastened above her knee. To everyone's delight she screamed and fell into her husband's arms, as though she had never heard of the joke *par excellence* of generations. The room rocked with the guests' merriment, and each was given a miniature garter of wax orange blossoms, ribbons and tiny bells, to wear on his coat. Then the singing began: ripe songs of experience dealt in the frankest way with married life, but no one was offended, for as the guests said, 'If you cannot discuss the functions of marriage at the marriage feast, where can you discuss them?'

Noble feasts have adorned weddings in very different circumstances: on the table at the Wilcox Log Tavern wedding in 1841, of William McElroy and Lucinda Collins, the first wedding ever to take place in Waupun, Wisconsin, there was 'a big gobbler, fattened for the occasion . . . a bowl of pickled cabbage, a dish of baked beans, a plate of boiled beets fantastically decorated with cloves, and after that the crowning dish of all – a glorious jelly cake, well seasoned with ginger, and molasses plentifully spread between the layers of jelly.'[47] By contrast with this cheerful improvisation, at the White House weddings of the same century bills of fare were printed on white satin and (at President Cleveland's wedding) the great floral ship *Hymen* sailed with silver-monogrammed white pennants in the State Dining-Room. Hollywood has been no less lavish. When Lana Turner married Bob Topping, life-sized statues of bride and groom carved from ice, and giant baked hams with 'I love you' spelled out on their sides with pimentos, greeted the guests.

There are special foods for weddings. The English 'bride's pie' with a laying hen and eggs, beneath a stout crust, was an essential dish, without which a couple had scant chance of happiness. At Cypriot weddings husband and wife eat roasted doves, birds which commonly decorate bridal chests. Doves were presented to the priest by Russian brides and were an auspicious gift for newlyweds in Cambridgeshire, to promote

A dove decoration for the wedding table, from Doves of Happiness, Inglewood, California (*Mrs Edie Steinmetz*)

their happiness. If doves are seen on the wedding day (especially if perching on the church roof) a harmonious home is assured. Number one of a limited edition of Royal Worcester porcelain white doves, after a model by Ronald van Ruyckevelt, were presented to Queen Elizabeth II and the Duke of Edinburgh for their silver wedding. This association of doves with weddings seems to be a clear survival of the cult of Venus.

Tradition is sustained by the Californian company Doves of Happiness, of Inglewood, which provides cooing and pirouetting white doves as decorations for weddings – many of socialites and show-business celebrities. Doves also appear at every wedding in the Doves of Happiness wedding chapel. Mrs Edie Steinmetz, who founded the business in 1959, says that for a dove to lay an egg at a wedding 'is considered the best luck in the world' and this fortunate event occurred at the Dean Martin–Cathy Hawn wedding, where thirty doves were on display in flower-decked cages flanking the entrance to the bridegroom's house, in tall 'gazebos', and in hanging baskets. For the wedding of Jack Lemmon and Felicia Farr, the florist decorated the doves' cages with fresh lemons. These doves all have names, which in 1973 included Fancy, Polly, Mr Barnaby and Yellowbird (retired, since she unfortunately suffered from car-sickness and could not go on assignment). The doves Princess Margaret and Lord Snowdon were hatched from eggs laid by doves on duty during a charity ball in Los Angeles attended by the royal couple. Doves of Happiness always rents doves in pairs to enhance romantic symbolism, and Mrs Steinmetz has discovered that people badly want the doves to coo at their weddings: birds of sufficient maturity must be chosen to ensure this. The flower-decorated cages of wrought iron may be shaped like wedding bells, or made to float upon the family swimming pool (as five cages did at the wedding of David Hemming and Gayle Hunnicutt).[48]

The ancient Greeks believed that the newly-married pair must eat a quince together to promote their love. The idea was long-lived: a family memorandum book noted that at a wedding in England in 1725 the bridegroom's grandfather presented the bride with a basket of quinces, to signify that in accepting a fruit both bitter and sweet she accepted her husband for better or worse. (The custom clearly showed Mediterranean origins: there the quince ripens fully and may be eaten raw, which does not occur in England.)

Nothing is more redolent of plenty than dairy produce. In seventeenth-century England, Thomas Moffett wrote: 'When the bride and bridegroom return home, one presents them with a pot of butter, as presaging plenty, and abundance of all good things.' And in Brittany an elaborate table ornament carved from butter – a knight on horseback, a church (so heavy that two of the farmer's men carried it in) or a flower-decorated crown – rested between the married pair at the feast.

Dancing and weddings have always gone together. At Glarus, by old custom, the first three dances were by bride and groom alone, so that village gossips could observe them closely and decide if lovemaking had been premature. Three musicians seated upon kitchen chairs played the flute, concertina and violoncello: by each stood an encouraging bottle of Veltliner, the local red wine. One young man, asked at what time he had got home to his mountain hut in the summer pastures, said 'In time for milking at dawn.' Wedding dancing required considerable fortitude from guests. A visitor to a Hungarian wedding in the late nineteenth century found the bride magnificent in a wreath of white roses, twenty petticoats and red boots. After a ten-course supper at which the visitor (called on for a contribution and not having a single word of Hungarian) proposed amid a storm of applause the old Gaelic toast *An la chi s-nach fhaix*, the dancing began, 'with every species of gymnastic dislocation . . .' Heel and toe, toe and heel, round whirled the dancers, clapping spurs and boots with their hands. The oldest dancer had seen service at the capture of Mantua in 1797 – but even he danced until dawn. At a wedding dance at New London, New Hampshire in 1769, sturdy and spirited guests completed a formidable programme of 92 jigs, 50 contra-dances, 43 minuets and 17 hornpipes; in Wales, the tune 'My Wife Shall Have Her Way' was reserved exclusively for wedding dancing. In Scotland it was the bride's privilege to choose the music for the 'shaim spring' which she danced with bridegroom, maids and best men.

Young people eagerly travelled many miles to a 'wedding

ball'. 'Straw boys' in disguising straw masks are distinctive visitors still seen occasionally at Irish weddings, treated with much respect, well entertained and claiming their ancient right to dance with the bride: they seem to be clear survivals of atavistic fertility and good-luck figures.

THE BIDDEN WEDDING

The wedding feast might stand alone and be given immediately after the ceremony, as is customary today. Or it might be part of the 'bidden wedding' or 'bridewain' which could be a wedding-day event or could be an entertainment held later, when the couple were established in their new home. There were many variants, but usually guests left money and gifts to provide the young people with a comfortable start in life; the term 'bidden wedding' conveyed rather more than the usual wedding invitation. In another fund-raising custom, seen in England until the seventeenth century, the bride herself might brew a strong 'bride-ale' (the origin of the word 'bridal') for sale to her friends and neighbours at a handsome price. Or a decorated 'bridewain' or waggon (in Yorkshire drawn by twenty oxen with beribboned horns) rolled through the villages collecting wood, corn, furniture and provisions for the newlyweds.

In Holland two bachelors with white ribboned wands summoned guests to bidden weddings, reciting the bill of fare in doggerel verse. Bidders in Wales were men of great personality. John Williams, bidder at Laugharne, Carmarthenshire, in the 1840s, made his round in a white apron with a white ribbon in his coat, a bidder's staff, and a bag swinging at his back for the bread and cheese given to him by farmers' wives on his long walk. His 'rammas' or invitation was long and witty, outlining the wedding meal and acceptable gifts – 'waggon or cart, cow and a calf, ox and a half' down to trivia such as cradles, fryingpans or mustard pots. 'A great many can help one, but one cannot help a great many,' went the rammas, enlarging on the bidding's philosophy. Bidders took pains to make the rammas entertaining, often adding a song and a dance: everything depended on its attracting guests.

The recipients of the presents kept careful accounts, for there was a binding obligation to repay bidding debts, which creditors could bestow upon the couple of their choice. The rammas might end with words such as: '. . . all payments due to the young woman's father and mother, grandfather and grandmother, aunts, brothers and sisters and the same due to the young man's father and mother etc., etc., must be returned to the young people on the above day . . .' The gifts were often delivered on the wedding eve and it seems plain that the custom is one of the origins of the American shower.

It was fully understood that guests' generosity (the non-debtors that is, since the rest were more or less obliged to give a present of a specified value) would at least partially depend on the entertainments. A gay and memorable occasion produced a richer haul. In 1796 one Cumberland bidding invitation set the scene with:

> Suspend for one day your cares and your labours,
> And come to this wedding, kind friends and good neighbours.

Another itemised the amusements:

> George Payton, who married Anne, the daughter of Joseph and Dinah Colin, of Crosby Mill, purposes having a Bride-wain at his house at Crosby, near Maryport, on Thursday, 7th day of May next (1789), where he will be happy to see his friends and well-wishers; for whose amusement there will be a variety of races, wrestling matches &c., &c. The prizes will be – a saddle, two bridles, a pair of *gânts d'amour*, which whoever wins, is sure to be married within the twelve months, a girdle (*ceinture de Venus*), possessing qualities not to be described; and many other articles, sports and pastimes . . .

In the evening the newlyweds would sit together to receive offerings from tired but happy guests. ('That you'll go home happy – as sure as a gun!' said another invitation, confidently.) They might be a hundred pounds better off by nightfall – and of course the gifts in kind were just as valuable to those setting up house.

In Scotland these occasions (noted for 'feasting, drinking,

dancing, wooing, fighting . . . always enjoyed with the highest relish' and, needless to say, roundly condemned by the church to no effect whatsoever) were known as 'penny bridals' or 'silver bridals', named from the guests' contributions. Gifts to the newly married, or towards the cost of the wedding feast itself, were made quite without embarrassment. In Salamanca, Spain, every guest who danced with the bride cut a slice of the pie which stood on her table – and left a coin under the crust; and at Breton wedding feasts the guests thrust cleft sticks holding coins into the butter table-ornament, until it resembled a porcupine.

Such customs are far from dead. At Polish weddings in New York's Lower East Side, the bride still dons a *babushka* in place of her wedding veil and dances with guests who pin dollar bills to her dress; the bridegroom also dances, wearing an apron with a large pocket for donations, and the lucky couple may collect several hundred dollars.

THE NEW HOME: CUSTOMS OF THE DOORSTEP

As the young bride left her father's house for the last time and said farewell to maiden life, there were special rites. Italian brides threw hot water over the threshold and the first of their unmarried sisters to mop it up would be first to marry. In Yorkshire too, boiling water was poured over the step and the bride dabbled her shoes in it to induce a happy marriage among the company, which would be arranged before the water was dry. As one cook said, as she hurried out with the kettle, 'We must keep the threshold warm for another bride!'

Today the entry of the newly-married pair into their home is divorced from magic. The honeymoon stands firmly between the wedding ceremony and this portentous moment. But when the two events took place on the same day, and when the wife looked forward only to a limited life within her home, emotions and supposed psychic dangers heightened the moment of entry. Doorsteps and thresholds, beloved of minatory spirits, were perilous for new wives. Unseen evil influences awaited them. Today, as a last remnant of the old precautionary rituals, a bride is carried over the threshold by her husband.

Fire, fertilising for crops, cattle and brides, installs the new life. In Spain a lighted candle awaits the pair and until at least 1870 a prophylactic smouldering peat was a doorstep safeguard for Scottish brides. In old China the bride was hoisted in over a glowing charcoal brazier; in Japan torches blazed on either side of the door and as the bride crossed the threshold two large candles, with wicks tied, were lighted and blown out, symbolising the hope that the couple would live in harmony, and die thus.

It is a moment for omens and good wishes. Good luck is certain if the sun shines on the door as the couple pass through. In Syria a lump of unleavened bread (for plenty), a green leaf (for fertility) and a silver coin (for wealth) are laid above the door, dates are scattered on the threshold and the bride washes her right heel in milk enabling her to step into her new life with abundance. Honey and yeast within the bride's hand ensures her sweetness to her husband, his prosperity. In Poland the father-in-law throws a handful of barleycorns over the newlyweds' heads and if the seeds germinate when planted in spring, all will go well for the pair.

Cake-breaking was formerly a widespread doorstep ritual. In Scotland, until at least 1900, a sieve of bread and cheese, or shortbread (*in-far-cake*), was broken over the bride's head and pieces carried away by the unmarried as 'dreaming bread'. A Yorkshire bride was given a cake on a plate: she ate a crumb or two and threw the remainder over her head, then passed the plate to her husband who tossed it over his head. Their future happiness depended upon its shattering and if by some grave mischance, it did not break, a watchful guest at once stamped upon it. The Yugoslavian bride hurled a *kolarh* cake of coarse dough over the house-roof: the higher it flew the greater her chances of happiness. Handling these staple foods, the daily diet, ensured that the couple would never want for them. Some saw the rituals as an echo of the Roman *confarreatio*, marriage by sharing bread, others as a passage rite, or symbolising the breaking of the bride's hymen, but whatever their purpose only a reckless couple scorned them.

Gods of hearth and household demanded appeasement at the arrival of the newly-made wife. In north-east Scotland a broom was placed in the bride's hand, the pothook from the fireplace swung three times round her head in the name of the Holy Trinity, and her hand thrust deep into the meal-chest, to the fervent prayer 'May the Almichty mack this unman a gweed wife' – a clear Christianising of a ritual of immemorial antiquity. Or the fire-irons were laid in her hands and she immediately mended the fire to emphasise continuity of hearth and home. Until recent years the Slavonian bride stirred the fire saying 'As many sparks spring up, so many cattle, so many male children, shall enliven the new home!' The Moroccan bride circles her home three times and in a ceremony full of pomp and dignity is told 'Thou shalt be the guardian of the hearth, and thou shalt stay as the peg of the tent.' Greek and Roman marriages originally took place not in the temple, but before the more powerful family hearth, where dwelt the deities of the household, the *lares* and *penates*. The Mordvin bride is led straight to the central stove to which she bows, beseeching it to love, obey and not to dirty her. Germans believed that the stove's mischievous spirit would tease the new wife unless an old woman pacified it by cooking the first meal of the marriage. Brides dropped coins and ribbons as propitiations in every corner of the house: even the well was not forgotten.

From crown prince to peasant, on the day after the wedding, Japanese couples formally report their marriage at the ancestors' shrine. Forbears crowd about newlyweds. In the Roman marriage ceremony the bride undertook the cult of her husband's gods, sacrificing to his ancestors to mark her incorporation into the new family, an ancient rite differing little from one encountered by a young man from Preston, Lancashire, at the end of the nineteenth century. He had married in London and took his bride home to visit his mother, whose first surprising question was 'Have you brought the wreath?', for in Lancashire it was customary for a new bride to lay a wreath on the family grave to show she was now a member of her husband's family. In Japan the stone *jizo* statue of the household god is carried in to the wedding feast, a bawdy verse pasted to his chest and a few days later he sits again in his accustomed niche by the pathway, wearing a smart new bib sewn by the new wife. It is said that he will stop her running home!

BEDDING THE BRIDE AND FLINGING THE STOCKING

Before the newly-married pair retired for the wedding night, sack-posset was served. *The New York Gazette*, 13 February 1744, gave the method of its making:

Receipt for all Young Ladies that are going to be Married
To make
SACK – POSSET

From famed Barbadoes on the Western Main,
Fetch sugar half a pound; fetch Sack from Spain
A pint; and from the Eastern Indian coast
Nutmeg, the glory of our Northern toast;
O'er flaming coals together let them heat
Till the all-conquering Sack dissolves the sweet.
O'er such another fire set eggs twice ten,
New born from foot of Cock and rump of Hen;
Stir them with steady hand, and conscience pricking,
To see the untimely fate of twenty chicken.
From shining shelf take down your brazen Skillet
A quart of milk from gentle cow will fill it:
When boiled and cooled, put milk and Sack to egg,
Unite them firmly like the Triple League.
Then cover close, together let them dwell
Till Miss twice sing: *You must not kiss and tell.*
Each lad and lass snatch up their murderous spoon,
And fall on fiercely like a starved Dragoon.

Then the couple attempted with greater or lesser success to creep away for the wedding night. In rural France the whole bridal party gaily hunted them like rabbits, firing guns triumphantly when their lair was discovered, and everyone rushed up to offer the traditional 'white soup' and cool cider to refresh them after their labours. Cambridgeshire weddings were great times for drinking and when bedtime came the pair were given final generous swigs of spirits before some sportsman shouted 'Off!' and, staggering, they lurched for the stairs. A spy reported on which reached bed first: if the bride, it proved she was a virgin!

In England, until the eighteenth century, the whole wedding party joined in 'bedding the bride'. The groom was put to bed by his men (with verbal and liquid encouragement), the bride by her maids, who carefully removed every pin from her dress – 'the prick of misfortune'. Even as late as 1896 it was said in Alabama to be unlucky to possess pins from a wedding dress, for they would cause lifelong spinsterhood. Wedding-night jokes and bawdy romps were usual at all levels of society, from court to cottage. Charles II personally drew the bed curtains when his niece Mary married William of Orange, saying bracingly to the nervous bridegroom, 'Now, nephew, to your work! Hey, St George for England!'

In Wales guests hung about the bridal chamber for days, drinking and singing full-blooded toasts to the newlyweds and their progeny, bridal chambers were invaded even in sober New England, where 'the entire company, regardless of the blushes or screams of the bride, marched round the nuptial couch, throwing old shoes, stockings and other missiles of established potency in such cases . . .'[49]

On both sides of the Atlantic 'flinging the stocking' was a favourite wedding-chamber sport: the men seized the bride's stockings and the girls the bridegroom's, and each group sat at the bed's foot in turn to toss the stockings over their heads to fall, for early marriage, on the bridegroom if thrown by a girl, on the bride if thrown by a man. The intention was explained thus:

> Then come all the younger folks in,
> With ceremony throw the stocking
> Backward, o'er head, in turn they toss'd it:
> Till in sack-posset they had lost it.
> Th'intent of flinging thus the hose
> Is to hit him or her on the nose,
> Who hits the mark o'er the left shoulder
> Must married be ere twelve months older.
>
> (*Progress of Matrimony*, 1733)

The American customs of throwing bouquet, garter and boutonnière are direct descendants of the old frolic of 'flinging the stocking'.

These lively bedroom sports, dependent upon the presence of the newlyweds, were common until about 1780: but, rather sadly, the increasing decorum of the later eighteenth and early nineteenth centuries and the growing popularity of wedding journeys and honeymoons (which after the days of capture had lapsed in favour of immediate entry into married life at home) brought about their end.

In the midst of the merriment, protective rituals were inevitably remembered. German brides sewed five crosses into their bridal quilts, against witches. Seven dates, seven leaves from seven fruit trees and a leaf of basil, stitched into the bridal mattress held the love of an Algerian husband. Scottish bridegrooms took care not to leave the bridal bed before their wives, or they would bear all the pains of childbirth. Whichever of the pair slept first on the wedding night would die first: the first to wake next day would be master of the household – and first to rise in the morning! The wedding-night candle was portentous: if it glowed red when blown out, all was well, but no glow showed that one of the pair had been unfaithful before marriage, and a grand row was only too likely before morning. A Moroccan marriage was always con-summated in a blaze of candlelight – so that the wife might appear to her husband 'as a shining light'.

Fertility was supremely important at this moment. In Ireland a hen about to lay an egg was tied to the bridal bedpost, or the couple were given a double-yolked egg to eat. A picture of fruit or flowers on the bridal-chamber wall and a piece of child's furniture about the room created a sympathetic atmosphere for rapid conception. In China five different coins of five different emperors nailed to the bridal bedstead guaranteed the couple at least twenty-five children! The Scottish bridal bed was always made up by a woman 'with milk in her breasts', for by imitative magic her handling of mattress and blankets 'magnetised' the bed for the couple about to occupy it.

In America and Britain today the consummation of marriages is little mentioned but such reticence is certainly not the case where virginity – and its evidence – are of great public interest. In Spain a cheerful crowd hangs below the bridal window singing spicy *coplas*, and when the bridegroom comes to the window to announce that all has gone well he is greeted with a great cheer, whistling and flag-waving. Since virginity usually affects the price asked for the bride, the bridegroom is naturally interested in the closer inspection of his bargain, and expects fair value for money. In many eastern Mediterranean countries the stained bridal nightdress and sheet flutter proudly from the nuptial window for several days for the village to admire and approve. There are good times or bad for consummation. In rural America, for example, consummation at or near the full moon is held to be particularly enjoyable, and in Cambridgeshire it was arranged if possible that the harvest moon of autumn should shine upon the bridal bed to fertilise the bride. In Spain it is said that only intercourse at the waxing moon will result in the conception of sons, and a family doctor in the English Midlands told the writer in 1975 that the week before he had been asked by three women patients if it were true that intercourse at the full moon invariably resulted in pregnancy. It is thought that as the moon has 'filled' so will the wife!

CHIVARI

If a widower married a girl much younger than he, or in village eyes a bereaved one remarried too hastily, the couple might be victims of chivari, an onomatopoeic name for the racket of tin cans, pots, pans and sheet iron, beaten below the couple's window by a hooting, shouting village rabble. In Spain, widows, fearful of humiliating *cencerrada*, rarely remarried, but one who did risk wedding her lover of many years was chivaried in fine style, with villagers meeting at the couple's farm to shout ribald verses and to bang upon their instruments. The victims wisely laid low, but after a time sent out their bailiff with a great jug of wine which he diplomatically handed round to the serenaders and the civil guard keeping a precautionary eye on events. As if by magic, this changed the whole mood of the party, and the offensive verses were quickly replaced by shouts of 'Olé, Olé' as the tormentors straggled happily homewards. When a barber in Seville, enthusiastic ringleader in many chivaris, himself married, the street outside the house was jammed on his wedding night with hundreds of his former victims, gathered by instinctive agreement to take a handsome and rackety revenge.

There were other wedding-night pranks practised by chivari-
ers. In *A Cornishman at Oxford*, 1965, A. L. Rowse, the historian,
remembered that in Cornwall his Uncle Harry and Aunt Polly
had found their door nailed up and chimney blocked when they
returned from their wedding. The joke was clearly erotic.
Chivari was perhaps introduced into America by the French of
Louisiana, or by emigrating Cornish miners: the young miners
of Fairplay near Dubuque, on the Wisconsin–Illinois border,
certainly welcomed the chance for chivari and kept the uproar
going until dawn. On one lively night the landlord of the
American House Tavern and his wife, finding the noise
unendurable, each rushed furiously from different doors of the
house with buckets of water to quell the riot. The collided in
the dark at the side of the inn and to everyone's delight, the
wife, without further enquiry, thoroughly doused her husband!

A similar uproar, 'rough music', 'riding the stang' or
'skimmington', greeted such misdemeanours of married life as
adultery, wifebeating, or nagging. (More liberal sexual
standards have happily removed at least one excuse for rough
music.) Rough music was often more a punishment of a

A 'rough music' procession. From Walker's *The Costume of Yorkshire*, 1814

compliant victim than of a wrongdoer, for by failing to play an appropriate sexual role he or she had jeopardised the collective wellbeing of the whole community. In a typical judgement, Breton fishermen tethered the luckless and henpecked husband to a cart, with a petticoat fluttering beside him, while in another cart rode the masterful wife, accompanied by a pair of trousers, to show that in this household at least, she wore them.

6

MARRIED LIFE

THE MORNING AFTER

The bridal night was short. Wellwishers not only bedded the couple but roused them at dawn. At Ste Ursule guests, still singing, marched home by starlight, yet everyone still wearing his replica bride's garter was ready at sunrise to thunder a lively reveille on the bridal door. Early on the day after the wedding the bride, still in bed, once received the *morgengabe* or 'morning gift' from her husband, to show his satisfaction with his bargain. When this had changed hands there was no returning her.

Scottish bridegrooms had a particularly trying day after the wedding. ''Tis a custom for the friends to endeavour the next day . . . to make the new-married man as drunk as possible,' wrote Allan Ramsay in 1721. 'Creeling' was a further ordeal. The bridegroom's friends fixed on his back a creel or basket full of stones (representing newly-assumed and weighty responsibilities). He was made to run round the town and was not allowed to drop his burden. His friends took good care that he did not! Only if the bride kissed him – and she might be a tease, or shy – was he released. The custom was self-perpetuating since the last man creeled was in charge and full of egalitarianism. But the custom, in Galashiels at least, was brought to a halt when about 1800 one Robert Young, on pretence of 'sore back', lay abed all day following his wedding, flatly refusing to rise to be creeled: he had been married twice before, he said, and had had more than enough of creeling!

'COMING-OUT BRIDE'

Wedding clothes were not quickly laid away. Before honeymoons became popular, on the Sunday following the wedding – known as 'Coming-Out Bride' in America,

'Showing-Off Sunday' in England – the whole bridal party in wedding finery appeared at church, arriving after the start of the service to give the congregation the best chance to view their splendours. They made their way majestically to the front pew or gallery, where during the sermon they rose to their feet and turned slowly about before admiring eyes. This display continued on each of the four honeymoon Sundays and the bride aimed at a new dress for each outing. At one Salem, Massachusetts, coming-out in 1810 the bride wore a delectable pink shirred plush bonnet, the bridegroom a matching pink plush hat and a coat of pink figured silk trimmed with pink plush. The men were no less gorgeous than the women.

Elsewhere too, similar customs allowed the couple to recapture the pleasurable theatricals of the wedding day, with none of its stresses. In Guernsey it was '*Reneurchounair*'; in Jersey the couple went to church to 'payi lûs r'gards' (presumably to a higher authority). In Ireland it was the 'Bride's Show'. On the way to church in England the husband walked in front to show he was master. As many as twenty-five couples might be married at Mardi Gras in the Plougastel peninsula and at the 'bragaden' on the following Sunday, couples in full finery arrived fifteen minutes late at mass to show off the men's fancy waistcoats of violet, green and white, beneath their red wedding jackets.

The bride was privileged to select the text for the 'Coming-Out Bride' sermon and there was much earnest searching. Ecclesiastes 4, 9, 10 was considered a good choice: 'Two are better than one; because they have a good reward for their labour. For if they fall, the one will lift up his fellow . . .' (A more cynical minister recommended Ephesians 6, 10, 11: 'Put on the whole armour of God . . .' – 'to teach that marriage is a state of warfaring contention'). A bridegroom appositely named Asa chose Chronicles 2, 14, 2, and he and his bride Hephzibah sat up proudly to hear 'And Asa did that which was good and right in the eyes of the Lord his God'. Until the eighteenth century English couples were regaled with the 'wedding psalm', 'Oh, well is thee, and happy shalt thou be' and the anthem 'Thy wife shall be as a fruitful vine'. Happiness and fertility were the great preoccupations.

The Dunmow flitch procession in 1751. The bacon, on a pole, is carried before the successful applicants, Thomas and Ann Shakeshaft, who sold slices of it among the crowd of 5,000. A print of C. Mosley 'from an original painting taken on the spot by David Ogborne'

THE DUNMOW FLITCH

If the marriage were successful the couple might apply for the 'Dunmow Flitch'. At least as early as the reign of King John, the monks of Dunmow Priory, Essex, England, established the prize of a flitch of bacon, awarded to a couple able to swear the traditional oath administered by the clerk of the manorial court, before a mixed jury of maidens and bachelors:

> You shall swear by Custom of Confession
> That you ne'er made nuptial transgression;
> Nor since you were married man and wife,
> By household brawls or contentious strife,
> Or otherwise, at bed, or at board,
> Offended each other in deed or in word;
> Or in a twelvemonth and a day,
> Repented not in thought any way;
> Or since the church clerk said 'Amen',
> Wished yourselves unmarried again,
> But continued true and in desire,
> As when you joined hands in holy quire.

Satisfactory respondents were given the bacon to the verse:

> Since to these conditions, without any fear,
> Of your own accord you do freely swear,
> A whole gammon of bacon you do receive,
> And bear it away with love and good leave;
> For this is the custom of Dunmow well known;
> Tho' the pleasure be ours — the bacon's your own!

The couple were then chaired and carried shoulder-high through the village, with the bacon on a pole going before.

In 1701 the court heard the claim of William Parsley, butcher, of Much Easton, and his wife Jane, married without ructions for three years. There were other applicants from time to time. Fifty years later Thomas Shakeshaft, a woolcomber of Wethersfield, showed sound business sense by selling slices of his gammon to the 5,000 spectators. Presentations followed sporadically into the nineteenth century: when Queen Victoria had been married to Prince Albert for a year and a day the lord of the manor boldly but confidently offered her the flitch. The gift was coolly declined. The queen was not amused.

The ritual had its imitators. In Yorkshire in the eighteenth century a dinner was arranged at the Green Dragon, Harrogate, for Mr and Mrs Liddal who, far from repenting of their union, confidently asserted that they could take the oath for the whole seventeen years of their married life. After a handsome repast the following poem circulated:

> Happy husband! Happy wife!
> Happy, happy both!
> Who, after a long married life,
> Could take the Flitch-of-Bacon oath!
> Which by all other couples fairly taken,
> How very few there are would 'save their bacon'.[50]

THE SALE OF WIVES

What if the union were found to be a mistake? The old remedy of wife-selling offered informal divorce to at least a section of the population until the late nineteenth century, and so deep-seated was it that popular indignation was great when Joshua Jackson was sentenced to imprisonment at the West Riding sessions in Yorkshire on 28 June 1837, for attempting a wife-sale. No one believed that he was breaking the law. Joseph Thomson, a Cumberland farmer, sold his wife in Carlisle market on 7 April 1832, with the regulation straw halter (an essential detail) about her neck. The halter 'validated' the deal. She was offered with the uninviting testimony that she was a 'born serpent' and a 'domestic curse', but her virtues were not overlooked: she could milk cows, read novels, make butter, scold maids and sing. A deal was clinched for twenty shillings and a Newfoundland dog. At Hereford market in 1876 the crowd advised a husband, bid only one shilling for his wife, to 'Keep her, master, keep her for her good looks,' but he retorted grimly, 'Good looks won't put victuals on the table without willing hands.'

Henry Frise of Lew Trenchard, Devon, bought his wife for half a crown at Okehampton market about 1840 and led her twelve miles home, watched in the final stages of the journey by a fascinated village. Despite remonstrances of parson and squire, Frise maintained stoutly: 'Her's my wife, as sure as if we was spliced at the altar. For and because I paid half a crown and never took off the halter till her was in my house!' When the 'wife' died about 1843 there was difficulty about the death registration: the parson would not and could not enter her as Anne Frise and after a heated argument Henry Frise, taking umbrage, buried his acquisition elsewhere.[51]

HAPPY ANNIVERSARIES

The custom of celebrating wedding anniversaries by name is apparently of German origin. Every wedding anniversary until the tenth has its motif; and thereafter named anniversaries occur at five-year intervals: the list varies (and may be expanded) but it usually reads:

first	paper	fourth	silk
second	cotton	fifth	wood
third	leather	sixth	iron

seventh	wool	thirtieth	pearl, ivory
eighth	bronze	thirty-fifth	coral
ninth	pottery	fortieth	ruby
tenth	tin	forty-fifth	sapphire
fifteenth	crystal	fiftieth	gold
twentieth	china	fifty-fifth	emerald
twenty-fifth	silver	sixtieth	diamond
		seventy-fifth	diamond

Since few couples can hope to reach their seventy-fifth wedding anniversary, the diamond wedding is usually celebrated after sixty years. Celebrants receive gifts of appropriate materials: the Ontario County Historical Society, New York, owns the complete set of tin articles given in 1867 to Mr and Mrs F. F. Thompson on their tenth wedding anniversary, a splendid blend of the practical and the humorous:

> Crown, spring bonnet, two stove-pipe hats, egg cooker and timer, strongbox, fruit dish, pipe, handmirror, rosary and crucifix, pudding mould, cookie cutters, tray, birdbath, watch and chain, playing cards, picture frames, lady's slippers, necktie, funnels, bookcovers, teaspoons, goblet, stein, fan, bric-a-brac shelves, toys, miniatures.

But in the main it is the silver, golden and diamond weddings which attract attention today. When on 20 November 1972 Queen Elizabeth II and the Duke of Edinburgh celebrated their silver wedding, they both received gifts of silver and gave them to others. A hundred couples also married on 20 November 1947 attended a service in Westminster Abbey with the royal couple, lunched at the Savoy Hotel and received silver dishes as mementoes.

American couples are sometimes given a tall white 'memory candle' which when lighted exudes a scent of lilies of the valley, a wedding flower. The candle is lighted at the couple's wedding reception and again at each anniversary. As it will burn for over 300 hours it will still be burning on the golden wedding day.

Sometimes the bride brings her wedding dress out for anniversary parties. President Hayes' wife wore her white silk dress at her silver wedding party at the White House in 1877, attended by the minister who had performed the marriage ceremony and family and friends from twenty-five years earlier. Often part of the wedding cake is laid away for these occasions, typifying the enduring qualities of marriage. In 1972 Mr and Mrs Eric Smith of Bournemouth, England, cut into the top tier of their wedding cake from forty years before: 'Over the years it had matured . . . and it all tasted delicious'; words, by fortunate chance, just as descriptive of a happy marriage.

REFERENCES

1 Huddleston, Sisley, *Between the River and the Hills; a Normandy Pastoral* (1931), 100–1
2 Thurston, E., *Ethnographic Notes in Southern India*, Madras (1906), 18–23; Wood-Martin, W.G., *Traces of the Elder Faiths of Ireland* (1902), 2, 34
3 Wilde, Lady, *Ancient Cures, Charms and Usages of Ireland* (1890), 47–8
4 Loftus, Charles, *My Life from 1815–49* (1877), 1, 302–3
5 *Wall Street Journal* (1 December 1974), 1, 27
6 Carr, John, *The Stranger in Ireland* (1807), quoted by Stiles, *Bundling*, 32
7 *Cottages of the Alps* (1860), 77, 91, 132
8 *Travels Through the Interior Parts of America: in a Series of Letters, (by an Officer)* (1781), 2, 37–40
9 *Sussex Notes and Queries*, 10 (1944), No 3, 59
10 Wright, Thomas, *The Romance of the Lace Pillow*, Olney (1931), 2, 148, 150–7, 256
11 *Daily Telegraph* (31 December 1974), 11
12 Lang, Olga, *Chinese Family and Society*, New Haven, Conn (1946), 123
13 Robacker, Earl F., *Touch of the Dutchland*, New York (1965), 163
14 Cole, H.E. ed, *Stagecoach and Tavern Tales of the Old Northwest*, ed Louise Phelps Kellogg, Cleveland, Ohio (1930), 266
15 *Church Times* (24 November 1893), 10
16 Saxon, Lyle, *Old Louisiana*, New York (1929), 283
17 Ovid, *Fasti*, trans J.G. Frazer (1902), 297
18 Devi, Rukmini, 'Railways Strike Halts Many Hindu Weddings', *Winnipeg Free Press* (5 September 1974), 19
19 Garnett, Lucy M.J., *The Women of Turkey and their Folk-Lore* (1890), 1, 242–3
20 *The Times* (3 July 1967), 4
21 O'Neill, Hannah Cox, *Devonshire Idylls* (1922), 203
22 *Globe and Mail* (17 July 1973), 10
23 Tromholt, Sophus, *Under the Rays of the Aurora Borealis: in the Land of the Lapps and Kraens* (1885), 1, 185–6
24 *Time* (14 June 1971), 14
25 Brown, William, *Britannia's Pastoral* (1613), 1, 2
26 Burne, Charlotte S., *Shropshire Folk-Lore: a Sheaf of Gleanings* (1883), reprinted Wakefield (1973–4), 1, 294

27 Blakeley, Godfrey, 'It Started with Teapot Handles', *Daily Telegraph Magazine* (4 January 1974), 10
28 Kames, Lord, *Sketches of the History of Man* (1813), 1, 449
29 Malkin, B.H. *Tour of South Wales* (1804), 67
30 *Bygones* (29 September 1897)
31 Von Reinsberg-Duringsfeld, I. and O., *Hochzeitsbuch* (1871), 246
32 Crawley, E., *The Mystic Rose*, New York (1902), 152
33 Seligman, C.G., *The Melanesians of British New Guinea* (1910), 268–9
34 Grey, Edwin, *Cottage Life in a Hertfordshire Village* (nd), 153–4
35 Schreiber, William I., *Our Amish Neighbours*, Chicago (1962), 194
36 *Daily Telegraph* (25 October 1974), 5
37 Scheftelowitz, I., 'Das Fischsymbol in Judentum und Christentum', *Archiv für Religionwissenschaft* (1911), 14, 377
38 Dewar, H.S.L., *The Giant of Cerne Abbas*, Guernsey (1968), 6–7
39 William Brown, Stockleigh Pomeroy, Devon, personal letter (11 September 1974)
40 Savory, Arthur H., *Grain and Chaff from an English Manor*, Oxford (1920), 94
41 Nicholson, John, *Folk Lore of East Yorkshire* (1890), reprinted Wakefield (1973), 3
42 Blakeborough, Richard, *Wit, Character, Folklore and Customs of the North Riding of Yorkshire* (1898), 100–1
43 Baring-Gould, Sabine, *A Book of Folk-Lore* (nd), 257–8
44 Vining, Elizabeth Gray, *Return to Japan*, New York (1960), 269
45 Beeton, Isabella, *The Book of Household Management* (1899), 1114
46 Duff, David, *Mother of the Queen* (1965), 68
47 Cole, H.E., *Stagecoach and Tavern Tales of the Old Northwest*, Cleveland, Ohio (1930). 267–8
48 Mrs Edie Steinmetz, Doves of Happiness, Inglewood, California; Blair, Kim, 'Laying Eggs a Coup in Dove Business', *Los Angeles Times* (3 June 1973)
49 Drake, Samuel Adams, *A Book of New England Legends and Folk Lore in Prose and Poetry*, Boston (1902), 209–10
50 *The Parlour Portfolio, Or, Post-Chaise Companion* (1820), 2, 111–2
51 Baring-Gould, S., *Devonshire Characters and Strange Events* (1908), 59–60

BIBLIOGRAPHY

Baker, Margaret, *The Folklore and Customs of Rural England*, Newton Abbot (1974)

Bentley, Marguerite, *Wedding Etiquette Complete*, New York (1964)

Brand, John, *Observations on the Popular Antiquities of Great Britain*, (1849), 3v

Chambers, R. ed, *The Book of Days, a Miscellany of Popular Antiquities*, (1862–4), 2v

Cole, Harry Ellsworth, ed, *Stagecoach and Tavern Tales of the Old Northwest*, Cleveland, Ohio (1930)

Crawley, E., *The Mystic Rose: A Study of Primitive Marriage and Primitive Thought in Its Bearing on Marriage*, New York (1902)

Daniels, Linn and Stevans, C.M., *Encyclopaedia of Superstitions, Folklore and the Occult Sciences of the World*, Milwaukee (1903), 3v

Earle, Alice Morse, *Customs and Fashions in Old New England*, New York (1904)

––––– *Two Centuries of Costume in America MDCXX–MDCCCXX*, New York (1902), 2v

Embree, John F., *Suye Mura: a Japanese Village*, Chicago (1939)

Epton, Nina, *Love and the Spanish* (1961)

Gantner, Theo, *Liebe und Hochzeit: Ausstellung im Schweizerischen Museum für Volkskunde, Basel 1972–3*, Basel (1973)

Garnett, Lucy M.J., and Stuart-Glennie, John S., *The Women of Turkey and Their Folk-Lore* (1890), 2v

Hone, William, ed, *The Table Book* (1864)

––––– ed, *The Year Book* (1864)

––––– ed, *The Every-Day Book* (1826–7), 2v

Johnson, W. Branch, *Folktales of Normandy* (1929)

––––– *Folktales of Brittany* (1927)

Legey, Françoise, *The Folklore of Morocco* (1935)

Leland, Charles, *Gypsy Sorcery and Fortune Telling* (1891), reprinted New York (1963)

McPherson, J.M., *Primitive Beliefs in the North-East of Scotland* (1929)

Morgenstern, Julian, *Rites of Birth, Marriage, Death and Kindred Occasions Among the Semites*, Cincinnati (1966)

Radford, E. and M.A. *Encyclopaedia of Superstitions*, ed and rev by Christina Hole (1961)

Randolph, Vance, *Ozark Magic and Folklore*, New York (1964)

Seligson, Marcia, *The Eternal Bliss Machine: America's Way of Wedding*,

New York (1973)

Singleton, Esther, *The Story of the White House*, New York (1907), 2v

Stiles, Henry Reed, *Bundling: Its Origin, Progress and Decline in America*, Albany (1871)

Tegg, W., *The Knot Tied: Marriage Ceremonies of All Nations* (1877), reprinted Detroit (1970)

Urlin, Ethel L., *A Short History of Marriage: Marriage Rites, Customs and Folklore in Many Countries and All Ages* (1913), reprinted Detroit (1969)

Van Gennep, Arnold, *The Rites of Passage*, trans Monika B. Vizedom and Gabrielle L. Caffee (1960)

PERIODICALS

Illustrated London News
Notes and Queries
Folklore (formerly *Folk-Lore*: *Folk-Lore Record*: *Folk-Lore Journal*)
Journal of American Folklore

ACKNOWLEDGEMENTS

I should like to thank the following for their kind assistance in the preparation of this book: George G. Harrap & Company Ltd for permission to quote from Sisley Huddleston's *Between the River and the Hills*; Mr Cecil Atkins, Waddesdon, Buckinghamshire; Mr A. J. M. Bannerman, Wessex Regional Office, The National Trust; Mr William Brown, Stockleigh Pomeroy, Devon; Mr and Mrs Adrian Dawes, Sittingbourne, Kent; Mr and Mrs Keith Emberson, Pembury, Kent; Mr David Evans, Westcott, Buckinghamshire; Miss B. D. Hadow, Moyses Stevens Ltd, London; Mrs Douglas Jennings, Toronto; Mrs Edie Steinmetz, Doves of Happiness, Inglewood, California; Mr Frank Vernon and the late Mrs Elsie Graver, Knutsford, Cheshire; Tiffany & Co, New York; Birmingham Museum & Art Gallery; Mr J. L. Howgego, Guildhall Library, London; The National Museum of Ireland, Dublin; The Trustees of the London Museum; The Metropolitan Museum of Art, New York; Dr Theo Gantner, Museum für Volkskunde, Basel; Norsk Folkemuseum, Oslo; the Victoria & Albert Museum, London; and finally, Mary Farnell of Wendover, Buckinghamshire, who prepared many of the photographs.

INDEX

Page numbers in italic type refer to illustrations